UNIX in a Nutshell

System V Edition

UNIX in a Nutshell

System V Edition

A Desktop Quick Reference

O'Reilly & Associates, Inc.
103 Morris Street, Suite A
Sebastopol, CA 95472

UNIX in a Nutshell: System V Edition

Editor: Tim O'Reilly

The following staff members of O'Reilly & Associates, Inc., worked on this
book: Jean Diaz, Dale Dougherty, Daniel Gilly, Linda Mui, Tim O'Reilly,
Thomas Van Raalte, Linda Walsh, Sue Willing, and Donna Woonteiler.
Special thanks to Cathy Brennan and Jill Berlin.

Printing History:

December 1986:	First edition.
September 1987:	Minor corrections.
February 1989:	Minor corrections.
October 1989:	Minor corrections.
May 1990:	Minor corrections.

ISBN: 0-937175-19-6   [2/92]

TABLE OF CONTENTS

1 UNIX Commands

Page

adb 1-2
admin 1-2
ar 1-3
as 1-4
asa 1-4
at 1-4
awk 1-5
banner 1-5
basename 1-5
basic 1-5
batch 1-6
bc 1-6
bdiff 1-6
bfs 1-6
cal 1-6
calendar 1-7
cancel 1-7
cat 1-7
cb 1-7
cc 1-8
cd 1-9
cdc 1-9
cflow 1-9
checkeq 1-9
checkmm 1-9
chgrp 1-10
chmod 1-10
chown 1-11
cmp 1-11
col 1-11
comb 1-12
comm 1-12
conv 1-12
cp 1-13

cpio 1-13
cpp 1-14
cprs 1-14
crontab 1-14
crypt 1-15
csplit 1-15
ct 1-16
ctcinfo 1-16
ctrace 1-16
cu 1-17
cut 1-19
cxref 1-19
date 1-19
dc 1-20
dd 1-20
delta 1-21
deroff 1-22
df 1-22
diff 1-22
diff3 1-23
diffmk 1-23
dircmp 1-23
dirname 1-24
dis 1-24
disable 1-24
du 1-25
dump 1-25
echo 1-26
ed 1-26
edit 1-26
efl 1-26
egrep 1-27
enable 1-27
enroll 1-27
env 1-27
eqn 1-27
ex 1-28
expr 1-28
f77 1-29
factor 1-30
false 1-30
fgrep 1-30

file 1-31
find 1-31
fsplit 1-33
ged 1-33
get 1-33
getopt 1-34
getopts 1-34
glossary 1-34
graph 1-34
graphics 1-35
greek 1-35
grep 1-36
help 1-36
helpadm 1-36
hp 1-36
hpio 1-36
hyphen 1-37
id 1-37
init 1-37
install 1-37
ipcrm 1-38
ipcs 1-38
ismpx 1-39
join 1-39
jterm 1-39
jwin 1-40
kill 1-40
layers 1-40
ld 1-41
lex 1-41
line 1-42
lint 1-42
list 1-42
ln 1-43
locate 1-43
login 1-43
logname 1-43
lorder 1-43
lp 1-43
lpstat 1-44
ls 1-44
m4 1-45

mail 1-46
mailx 1-46
make 1-47
makekey 1-48
man 1-48
mesg 1-48
mkdir 1-48
mknod 1-48
mm 1-49
mmt 1-49
mount 1-49
mv 1-49
newform 1-50
newgrp 1-51
news 1-51
nice 1-51
nl 1-51
nm 1-52
nohup 1-53
nroff 1-53
od 1-54
pack 1-54
passwd 1-54
paste 1-54
pcat 1-55
pg 1-55
pic 1-55
pr 1-56
prof 1-56
prs 1-57
ps 1-57
ptx 1-58
pwd 1-58
pxp 1-59
ratfor 1-59
red 1-59
refer 1-60
regcmp 1-60
rm 1-60
rmdel 1-61
rmdir 1-61
rsh 1-61

sact 1-61
sag 1-61
sar 1-62
scat 1-63
scc 1-63
sccsdiff 1-63
sdb 1-63
sdiff 1-64
sed 1-64
setup 1-65
sh 1-65
shl 1-65
shutdown 1-66
size 1-66
sleep 1-66
sort 1-67
spell 1-67
spline 1-68
split 1-68
starter 1-68
strip 1-68
stty 1-69
su 1-72
sum 1-73
sync 1-73
sysadm 1-73
tabs 1-73
tail 1-74
tar 1-74
tbl 1-75
tc 1-75
tee 1-75
test 1-75
time 1-75
timex 1-76
touch 1-76
tplot 1-76
tput 1-77
tr 1-77
troff 1-77
true 1-78
tsort 1-78

tty 1-78
umask 1-78
umount 1-78
uname 1-79
unget 1-79
uniq 1-79
units 1-80
unpack 1-80
usage 1-80
uucp 1-80
uulog 1-81
uuname 1-81
uupick 1-81
uustat 1-82
uuto 1-82
uux 1-82
val 1-83
vc 1-84
vedit 1-84
vi 1-84
view 1-85
wait 1-85
wall 1-85
wc 1-85
what 1-85
who 1-85
write 1-86
xargs 1-86
yacc 1-87

2 Shell Syntax

The Bourne Shell 2-2
The C Shell 2-12
The Bourne Shell vs. The C Shell 2-26

3 Pattern Matching

Metacharacters 3-2
Pattern Matching Examples 3-3

4 Editor Command Summary

The vi Editor 4-2
The ex Editor 4-14
The sed Editor 4-26
awk 4-32

5 Nroff and Troff

Nroff/Troff Requests 5-3
Escape Sequences 5-17
Predefined Number Registers 5-19
Special Characters 5-21

6 Macro Packages

-mm Macros 6-2
-ms Macros 6-23
-me Macros 6-33

7 Preprocessors

tbl 7-2
eqn 7-6
pic 7-10

8 Program Debugging

The adb Debugging Program 8-2
The sdb Debugging Program 8-7

9 SCCS and Make

SCCS 9-2
The MAKE Utility 9-7

UNIX in a Nutshell

1

UNIX Commands

This section includes a description of each command found in Section 1 of the *UNIX Programmer's Manual*. The command syntax is followed by a brief description of the command's function and a list of all available options, as described in Releases 2.0 through 3.3 of System V.

The conventions used in this section are as follows:

- All commands and options shown in **boldface** are typed literally.

- All arguments and options shown in *italics* are generic and should be replaced with user-supplied values.

- All arguments surrounded with brackets are optional. Note that many commands show the argument [*file(s)*]. If a filename is omitted, standard input (i.e., the keyboard) is assumed. End with an EOF character (normally ^D).

- The syntax line should be entered as shown, including blank spaces. Note for example that an option shown as **-w***n* (the numeric argument *n* follows the -w flag with no intervening whitespace) is different from **-w** *n*.

- A ☞ at the bottom of a right-hand page means that the listing for the current command is continued on the next page.

adb	**adb** [*option*] [*objfile* [*corefile*]]

A general purpose debugging program used to look at "core" files resulting from aborted programs. *objfile* contains an executable program and *corefile* contains the core image produced when *objfile* executed. **a.out** is the default *objfile*. **core** is the default *corefile*. See Section 8 for more information on **adb**.

options

    -w   create both *objfile* and *corefile* and open for modification. |
| **admin** | **admin** [*options*] *files*

Add *files* to SCCS or change *options* of SCCS *files*. See Section 9 for more information on SCCS.

options

  -a*user*\|*groupid*
      assign *user* or *groupid* permission to make deltas.
  -d*flag*[*value*]
      delete *flag* set previously with **-f** flag. Values for *flag* are the same as described for the **-f** option below.
  -e*user*
      take away delta privileges from *user*.
  -f*flag*[*value*]
      set *flag* with optional *value*. Applicable *flags* and *values* are as follows: |

b	allow branch deltas.
c*n*	set highest release to *n* (default is 9999).
f*n*	set lowest release to *n* (default is 1).
d*n*	set **get** default delta number.
i[*string*]	treat "No id keywords (ge6)" as a fatal error. *string*, if present, forces a fatal error if keywords do not exactly match *string*.
j	allow multiple concurrent **gets**.
l*list*	releases in *list* cannot accept changes.

n	create a null delta.
q *string*	substitute %Q% keyword with *string*.
m *name*	substitute %M% keyword with module *name*.
t *type*	substitute %Y% keyword with module *type*.
v [*file*]	prompt for modification request number as the reason for creating a delta.

admin
continued

- **-h**   check the SCCS file structure.
- **-i** [*file*]
  - use *file* as source for a new SCCS file.
- **-m** [*list*]
  - insert *list* of modification request numbers.
- **-n**   create a new SCCS file.
- **-r** *n.n*   set initial delta to release number *n.n*.
- **-t** [*file*]
  - take descriptive text from *file*.
- **-y** [*text*]
  - insert *text* as comment for initial delta (only valid with **-i** or **-n**).
- **-z**   recompute the SCCS file checksum and store in first line.

---

ar *key* [*posname*] *archive files*

ar

Maintain a group of *files* that are combined into *archive*. Used most commonly to create and update library files as used by the link editor

key

a	after *posname* (used with **r** or **m**).
b	before *posname* (used with **r** or **m**).
c	create *archive* silently.
d	delete *files* from *archive*.
i	before *posname* (used with **r** or **m**).
l	place temporary files in local directory rather than **/tmp**.
m	move *files* to end of *archive*.
p	print *files* in *archive*.
q	append *files* to *archive*.
r [u]	replace *files* or, optionally, only files modified later than *archive*.

ar	**s**	force regeneration of *archive* symbol table
continued	**t**	print table of contents for *archive*.
	v	verbose, print a description.
	x	extract *files* from *archive*.

posname

Name of a file used to indicate the position in *archive*. Must be preceded by: **a**(after), **b** or **i** (before).

---

as

as [*options*] *file*

Assemble the specified assembler source *file* and place the result in a file called **a.out**.

options

    -m   run **m4** on the input.
    -n   turn optimization off.
    -o *objfile*
        place output in *objfile* (default is **a.out**).
    -R   remove *file* upon completion.
    -V   print the version number of *list*.

There may be additional system-specific options.

---

asa

asa *files*

Process FORTRAN output files that contain ASA carriage control characters and print the result on standard output. **asa** uses the first character of each line for format control; this character is not printed.

---

at

at *time* [*date*] [+ *increment*]
at *option* [*job*]

Execute commands entered on standard input at a specified *time* and optional *date*. If *file* not specified, read commands from standard input; end with **^D**.

time

hour (hh), minute (mm), and optional **a**(am), **p**(pm), **m**(midnight), or **n**(noon) (e.g., *230p* is the same as *1530*).

date
month name followed by a day number (e.g., *jan 24*) or a day of the week (e.g., *jan mon*). Add the word "week," and the command is executed a week later (e.g., *jan mon week*).
options
 	
  -r   Removes all previously scheduled jobs.
  -l   Reports all jobs scheduled for the invoking user.
	at
	continued

awk [*options*] [*program*] [*parameters*] [*files*]
 	
Use the pattern-matching "*program*" to modify the specified *files*. See Section 4 for more information on **awk**.
options
 	
  -f*file* use patterns contained in *file*.
  -F*c*   separate fields with character *c*.
 	
parameters
awk accepts *parameters* such as x= . . . y= . . . on the input line.
	awk

banner *chars* Print *chars* as a poster on the standard output.	**banner**
basename *pathname* [*suffix*] Remove the path prefix *pathname* and optional *suffix* (e.g. **.c**) and print the resulting filename on standard output. See also **dirname**.	**basename**

basic [*options*] [*file*]
 	
Interpret and run the BASIC language program contained in *file*.
options
 	
  -n   load the program but do not run it.
  -s *size* set the size of the memory reserved for the user work space.
	basic

batch	**batch** Execute commands entered on standard input. Unlike **at**, which will execute commands at a specific time, **batch** executes commands when system load permits. End with ^D.

bc	**bc** [*options*] [*files*]
	
	Perform precision arithmetic interactively. Input can be taken from *files* or read from the standard input.
	
	options
	
	   -c do not invoke **dc**, compile only.
	   -l use arbitrary precision math library.

bdiff	**bdiff** *file1 file2* [*options*]
	
	Compare *file1* with *file2* and report the differing lines. This command is used for files containing too many lines for **diff**. See also **diff**.
	
	options
	
	   n split each file into *n*-line segments (default is 3500).
	   -s suppress error messages.

bfs	**bfs** [*option*] *file* Big file scanner — reads a large *file*, using **ed**-like syntax. This command is more efficient than **ed** for scanning very large files because the file is not read into a buffer. Files can be up to 1024k. **bfs** can be used to view a large file and identify sections to be divided with **split** or **csplit**. *option* **-** do not print the file size.
cal	**cal** [[*month*] *year*] Print a 12-month calendar for the specified *year* or a single *month*. Without options, print calendar for the current month.

options

> *month* a digit (1-12) specifying the month (e.g., *cal 12 1984*).
>
> *year*   a digit (1-9999) specifying the year (e.g., *cal 1984*).

---

calendar [-]

calendar

Read the "calendar" file, located in your home directory, and send all lines (via mail) that contain the current date.

option

> -   invoke calendar for all users.

---

cancel [*id*] [*printer*]

cancel

Cancel the print request *id*(s), or the print request currently printing on *printer*. Use **lpstat** to determine either the *id* or the *printer* to cancel.

---

cat [*options*] [*files*]

cat

Read and print one or more *files*. Several files may be combined and directed to another file with the ">" operator (*e.g., cat ch1 ch2 ch3 > book*). To avoid overwriting any files, the new filename must be different from the filenames to be combined. If no files are specified, read from standard input; end with ^D.

options

> -s   suppress the "Non-existent File" message.
> -u   do not buffer output.
> -v   print non-printing characters (except tabs, new-lines and form-feeds).
>   Options used with -v:
> -e   print a "$" prior to a newline.
> -t   print "^I's" instead of tabs.

---

cb [*files*]

cb

C program "beautifier" that formats *files* using proper C programming structure.

☞

---

cb
continued

options

-**j**   join split lines.

-**l** *length*
     split lines longer than *length*.

-**s**   standardize code to style of Kernighan and Ritchie in *The C Programming Language*.

---

cc

cc [*options*] *files*

Compile one or more C (*file*.c) or assembler (*file*.s) source files. Output is placed in **a.out** by default.

options

-**B***directory*
     use *directory* in place of the default directory containing the preprocessor, compiler, assembler, or link editor.

-**c**   suppress the loading phase.

-**E**   run only the macro preprocessor.

-**f**   use the floating-point interpreter.

-**g**   generate the symbol table information needed for the debugger.

-**O**   optimize the code.

-**p**   generate benchmark code to count the times each routine is called.

-**P**   run only preprocessor and place the result in *file*.**i**.

-**S**   place assembler output in *file*.**s**.

-**t** [p012al]
     replace only the specified phase of the compilation with the programs found in the alternate directory chosen with the -**B** option.

-**W** [p012al] *arg1* [*arg2* ...]
     hand off the arguments *argi* to pass the specified phase of the compilation.

-**y** *limit*
     specify the text size increase *limit*. Valid *limits* are:

     u - unlimited

     n - an integer

     s - no expansion

There may be additional system-specific options.

cd [*directory*]   **cd**

Change the current working directory to *directory*. If *directory* not specified, change to user's home directory.

---

cdc [*options*] *files*   **cdc**

Change the delta comments for one or more SCCS *files*. See Section 9 for more information on SCCS.

options

    -m [*list*]
        add the *list* of modification request numbers.

    -r *sid* SCCS delta id version number.

    -y [*string*]
        replace comment with *string*.

---

cflow [*options*] *files*   **cflow**

Build an external reference graph for the C, LEX, YACC, assembler, or object *files*.

options

    -d *n* cut off the graph at depth *n*.

    -i_   include procedures whose names begin with "_".

    -ix include external and static procedures.

    -r   produce an inverted listing showing the callers of each function, sorted in lexographical order by callee.

---

checkeq [*files*]   **checkeq**

Report missing or unbalanced delimiters for *eqn* in *files*.

---

checkmm [*files*]   **checkmm**

Check *files* for **mm** errors.

---

chgrp	**chgrp** *newgroup files*
	Change the ownership of one or more *files* to *newgroup*. *newgroup* is either a group id number or a group name defined in /etc/group.
chmod	**chmod** *permission files*
	Change the access mode of one or more *files*. Only the owner of a file or a superuser may change its mode.
	Create *permission* by concatenating members of *who*, *opcode*, and *mode*.

who

u	user.
g	group.
o	other.
a	all.

opcode

+	add permission.
-	remove permission.
=	assign permission.

mode

r	read.
w	write.
x	execute.
s	set user (or group) id.
t	save text (sticky) mode.
u	user's present permission.
g	group's present permission.
o	other's present permission.

For example, **chmod u+x** *file* will add execute-by-user permission to *file*.

Alternatively, specify permissions by a 3-digit sequence. The first digit designates owner permission; the second, group permission; and the third, others permission. Digits are calculated as a compilation of the following values:

4 read
2 write
1 execute

For example, **chmod 751** *file* makes *file* read-write-execute by owner, read-execute by group, and execute-only for others.

chmod
continued

---

chown *newowner files*

chown

Change the ownership of one or more *files* to *newowner*. *newowner* is either a user id number or a login name located in **/etc/passwd**.

---

cmp [*options*] *file1 file2*

cmp

Compare *file1* with *file2* and print the differing byte and line numbers.

options

-l   print byte number and differing bytes.
-s   print only the return codes:
        0 = files are identical.
        1 = files are different.
        2 = files are inaccessible.

---

col [*options*]

col

Perform line overlays as specified by reverse line-feeds and by forward and reverse half-line feeds. Useful for filtering output produced by the **.rt** command of **nroff** or by **tbl**.

options

-b   assume that the output device cannot perform backspacing; therefore, print only the last of several characters that must appear in the same place.
-f   produce output that contains forward half-line-feeds but no reverse line motion.
-p   print unknown escape sequences (normally ignored) as regular characters. Use of this option requires full awareness of the textual position of the escape sequences.
-x   do not convert white space to output tabs.

comb	**comb** [*options*] *files*

Combine SCCS deltas of the named *files*. See Section 9 for more information on SCCS.

options

   -c*list* preserve the deltas in *list*. *list* syntax can be found under **get**.

   -o   access "as created" file instead of most recent.

   -p*sid* oldest delta version number to be preserved.

   -s   generate a shell file which prints space savings data.

---

comm

comm [*options*] *file1 file2*

Compare lines common to the sorted files *file1* and *file2*. Three-column output is produced with each column containing either lines only in *file1*, lines only in *file2*, or lines in both *files*.

options

   -   read the standard input.

   -1   suppress printing of column 1.

   -2   suppress printing of column 2.

   -3   suppress printing of column 3.

   -12   print only the lines common to *file1* and *file2*.

   -23   print only the lines in *file1* but not *file2*.

---

conv

conv [*options*] *files*

Convert the object *files* so that they conform to the standards of another version of UNIX. The output for each file is sent to *file*.**v**.

options

   -   take input from standard input.

   -a   produce output in UNIX System V 2.0 portable format.

   -o   for archives, output is produced in the old format.

   -p   for archives, output is produced in UNIX System V Release 1.0 format.

-t *target*
> produce output for *target*.
>
> *target* is one of:
> b16, ibm, i80, m32, mc68, n3b, pdp

There may be additional system-specific options.

conv
continued

---

cp *file1 file2*
cp [**-f**] *files directory*

cp

Copy *file1* to *file2*, or copy one or more files to specified directory under same name. If destination file already exists, it will be overwritten.

option

    -f   copy unconditionally

---

cpio *options flags*

cpio

Copy file archives in or out from tape or disk. Each of the three options has different flags, as follows:

cpio -o [**aBcv**]
Copy out a list of files whose names are given on the standard input.

cpio -i [**bBcdmrsStuv**] [*patterns*]
Copy in files whose names match selected *patterns* in the style of **sh** and **csh**. (Patterns should be quoted or escaped so they are interpreted by **cpio**, not the shell.)

cpio -p [**adlmruv**] *directory*
Copy files to another directory on the same system. Destination pathnames are interpreted relative to the named *directory*.

flags

a	reset access times of input files.
b	swap bytes and halfwords.
B	block input/output 5120 bytes/record.
c	write header information as ASCII characters.
d	create directories as needed.
f	all files are copied except those in *patterns*
l	link rather than copy files.
m	retain previous file modification time.

☞

cpio *continued*	**r**	rename files interactively.
	s	swap bytes.
	S	swap halfwords.
	t	print a table of contents of the input (no files created). When used with the −v option, resembles output of **ls −l**.
	v	print a list of file names.

cpp

cpp [*options*] [*ifile*] [*ofile*]

The **cpp** command runs the C preprocessor on the input file *ifile* and places the output in *ofile*.

options

    -C   do not strip comments.

    -D*name*[*=def*]

        define the *name* to the C preprocessor with the value *def*, or 1 if *def* is not specified.

    -H   print the include files on standard output.

    -I*dir*   include the directory *dir* in the include file search path.

    -P   do not produce the line control information for the next pass of the C compiler.

    -T   use only the first eight characters to distinguish preprocessor names.

    -U   remove any initial definition of *name*, where *name* is a predefined reserved symbol.

cprs

cprs [*options*] *objfile file*

Compress object file *objfile* and put output in *file*.

options

    -p   produce compression statistics.

    -v   print error messages in long form.

crontab

crontab [*options*] *file*

Add or delete a *file* from the crontab directory.

options

    -l   list the user's file in the crontab directory.

-r   delete the user's file in the crontab directory.

Each line in *file* should contain the following fields.
An asterisk in any time field means all possible values.

minute:	(0-59)
hour:	(0-23)
day_of_month:	(1-31)
month:	(1-12)
day_of_week:	(0-6)
command	

crontab
continued

---

crypt [*password*] < *file* > *encryptedfile*

Encrypt a *file* to prevent unauthorized access. The
same *password* is used to encrypt a file or decrypt an
encrypted file. If no password is specified, **crypt**
prompts for one.

crypt

---

csplit [*options*] *file arguments*

Separate a *file* into sections and place in *file*xx00
through *file*xx*n*, *n* < 100, breaking the file at each pattern specified in *arguments*.

options

    -f *file* name new files *file*00 through *filen* (default
        is **xx00** through **xx***n*).

    -k   leave previously created files intact.

    -s   suppress all character counts.

arguments

Any one or a combination of the following expressions:

    /expr/ create file from the current line up to the
        line containing the regular expression *expr*.

    %expr%

        same as */expr/* except no file is created for
        lines previous to line containing *expr*.

    n   create a file from the current line up to line
        number *n*.

    {n} repeat argument *n* times. May follow any
        of the above arguments.

csplit

---

ct	**ct** [*options*] *telno*

Initiate a **getty** on a remote terminal. *telno* is the telephone number of the modem to which the terminal is attached. Equal signs wait for a secondary dial tone; minus signs give a brief pause.

options

- **-h** prevent automatic hangup on the line.
- **-s***speed*
      set the baud rate to *speed*.
- **-v** verbose error reporting.
- **-w***n* set *n* as maximum number of minutes to wait for a line.
- **-x***n* set the debug level to *n*. Level 9 is recommended.

---

ctcinfo

ctcinfo [*options*]

Provide information for a cartridge tape.

options

- **-a** print total number of bytes.
- **-b** number of bytes per cylinder.
- **-B** total number of blocks on tape.
- **-c** number of cylinders.
- **-d** device type.
- **-m** maximum tape pass count.
- **-s** number of sectors per track.
- **-t** tape pass count.
- **-u** tape drive usage count.
- **-v** volume table of contents.
- **-x** number of tracks per cylinder.

special option

- **-r** reset the usage count. Use only when the tape is cleaned.

---

ctrace

ctrace [*options*] [*file*]

Debug a C program. **ctrace** reads the C source file in *file* and writes a modified version to standard out.

options

ctrace
continued

    -b   only trace the basic C functions.

    -e   print variables with floating point format.

    -f*functions*

            trace just the specified *functions*.

    -l*n*   loop *n* times (default 20).

    -o   print variables with hexadecimal format.

    -p´*s*´ use the function *s* as the trace function (default 'prinf(').

    -P   run the C preprocessor.

    -r*file* change trace package from the default *run-time*.c to *file*.

    -s   suppress certain redundant code.

    -t*n*   trace *n* variables.

    -u   print variables with unsigned format.

    -v*functions*

            do not trace listed *functions*.

    -x   print variables with floating point format.

---

cu [*options*] *telno* | *dir* | *system*

cu

Call up another UNIX system or a terminal via a direct line or a modem. A non-UNIX system can also be called. When a *system* is known to **uucp**, the command "**cu** *system*" handles the connect options.

options

    -d   print diagnostics.

    -e   use even parity.

    -l*line* *line* is the name of the communications line device (e.g. /dev/tty001).

    -h   emulates local echo and supports calls to other computer systems which expect terminals to be in half duplex mode.

    -o   use odd parity.

    -s*speed*

            set the baud rate to *speed*.

    -t   dial an ASCII terminal with auto answer set (see **ct**).

    telno the telephone number. Equal signs wait for a secondary dial tone; minus signs give a brief pause.

    system

            call the *system* known to **uucp**.

☞

cu runs as two processes: transmit and receive. Transmit reads from standard input and passes lines to the remote system (except lines beginning with " "). Receive reads data from the remote system (except lines beginning with " ").

Transmit options:

~.   terminate the conversation.

~!   escape to an interactive shell on the local system.

~*cmd* ...

    run command on local system (via **sh -c**).

~$*cmd* ...

    run command locally and send output to remote system.

~%take *file* [*target*]

    copy *file* from remote system to *target* on the local system.

~%put *file* [*target*]

    copy *file* from the local system to *target* on the remote system. If *target* is omitted *file* is used in both places.

~ ~ ...

    send the line ~ ... to remote system. Use to issue commands to more than one systsem in a **cu** chain. E.g., use ~~. to terminate the conversation on a second system **cu**'d to from the first.

~%break

    send BREAK sequence to remote system.

~%debug

    turn debug mode on.

~%l   print termio structure variables for the line out.

~%nostop

    turn off the DC3/DC1 (^S, ^Q) input control protocol for the remainder of the session.

~%t   print the termio structure for the local terminal.

To redirect the output of the Receive process from the standard output to a file use the following sequence:

~>[>]:*file*
zero or more lines to be written to file.

~ >

divert (or append, if >> is used) to *file*. The
trailing ˜ > terminates the diversion.

cu
continued

The file **/usr/lib/uucp/L-devices** is consulted. The file
/usr/spool/uucp/LCK..(*tty-device*) is the lock file.

---

cut *options* [*files*]

cut

Select a list of columns or fields from one or more
files. Either the **-c** or **-f** option must be specified.

options

   -c*list*   a comma-separated *list* of column posi-
           tions, where *list* is any specified column or
           range of columns (e.g. 1-9,11 or 3,5-).

   -d*c*   field delimiter character is *c* (default is tab).

   -f*list* a comma-separated *list* of fields, where *list*
           is any specified column or range of col-
           umns (e.g. 1-9,11,13-).

   -s   suppress lines without delimiters.

---

cxref [*options*] *files*

cxref

Build a C cross-reference table for the specified C
source *files*.

options

   -c   combine the cross-reference list for all
           files.

   -o *file* send output to *file*.

   -s   do not print input file names.

   -t   format for 80-column listing.

   -w*num*
           format width no wider than *num*. If *num* is
           less than 51 or not specified, default is 80.

---

date [*mmddhhmm*[*yy*]] [+*format*]

date

Display the current date and time in *yymmddhhmm.ss*
format. A superuser may set the date and time with a
specified *format*, as listed below.

☞

date *continued*	*mm* month number (e.g., *12*). *dd* day number (e.g., *25*). *hhmm* hour and minute (24-hour clock). [*yy*] last two digits of the year (e.g., *84*).

format

a	abbreviated weekday.
d	day of month (01-31).
h	abbreviated month (Jan-Dec).
j	julian date (001-366).
m	month of year (01-12).
n	insert a newline character.
r	time in am/pm notation.
t	insert a tab character.
w	day of week (Sunday = 0).
y	last two digits of the year (00-99).
D	date, in mm/dd/yy format.
H	hour (00-23).
M	minute (00-59).
S	second (00-59).
T	time, in hh:mm:ss format.

If *format* begins with +, output of date is under the control of the user.

---

dc

dc [*file*]

An interactive desk calculator program that performs integer arithmetic (input may be taken from a *file*). The input and output number base, as well as the number of fractional digits, can be specified by the user.

---

dd

dd [*options*]

Make a copy of an input file with the specified conversions and send the results to the output file, or standard output if **of** is not specified.

options

bs=*n*	set input and output block size to *n* bytes.	
cbs=*n*	set conversion buffer size to *n*.	
conv	=ascii	EBCDIC to ASCII.
	=block	variable to fixed length records.

=ebcdic	ASCII to EBCDIC.
=ibm	ASCII to EBCDIC with IBM conventions.
=lcase	upper case to lower case.
=noerror	continue when an error occurs.
=swab	swap all pairs of bytes.
=sync	pad input records to **ibs**.
=ucase	lower case to upper case.
=unblock	fixed records become variable length.
=...,...	more than one conversion, comma-separated.

count=*n*
> copy only *n* input records.

files=*n*
> skip *n* input files.

ibs=*n* set input block size to *n* bytes (default is 512).

if=*file* input filename is *file* (default is standard input).

obs=*n* set output block size to *n* bytes (default is 512).

of=*file*
> output to *file* (default is standard output).

seek=*n*
> seek *n* records from start of output file.

skip=*n*
> skip *n* input records.

The output is written as if filtered through "od -c". It is blocked by "input record". If *tape* is specified also, that information will precede each block dumped. This may be useful when examining unknown tapes.

---

delta [*options*] *files*

delta

Incorporate changes to one or more SCCS *files*. See Section 9 for more information on SCCS.

options

> **-g***list* ignore deltas in *list*.
> **-m** [*list*]
>> *list* of modification request numbers.

☞

delta *continued*	**-n** save changes file *file*.**g**. **-p** print delta references. **-r** *sid* delta version number. **-s** suppress printing of new SCCS id. **-y**[*string*] insert *string* as a comment.

deroff

deroff [*options*] [*files*]

Remove all **nroff**, **troff**, **tbl**, and **eqn** requests from the named *files*.

options

    -i   ignore ".so" and ".nx" commands.
    -ml   delete **mm** macro lists.
    -mm ignore text from mm macro lines.
    -w   output only one word per line.

df

df [*options*] [*name*]

Report number of free disk blocks and i-nodes.

options

    -l   report only on local file systems.
    -t   report total allocated space as well as free space.
    -f   report free blocks but not free i-nodes.

name can be a device name, a mount point directory name, a directory name, or a remote resource name.

diff

diff [*options*] *file1 file2*
diff [*diroptions*] *dir1 dir2*

Report the lines that differ between *file1* and *file2*, or if *diroptions* are specified, report the files that differ between *dir1* and *dir2*.

options

    -b   ignore blank spaces and tabs.
    -c*n*   produce *n* lines of context (default is 3).
    -e   produce a script of commands to recreate *file2* from *file1* using the **ed** editor.
    -f   produce a script to recreate *file1* from *file2* but not in reverse order required by **ed**.

-h   perform the comparison quickly.
 	
diroptions
 	
    -l   long output format.
    -r   recursive **diff** for common subdirectories.
    -s   report files that are identical.
    -S*file* begin directory comparison with *file*.
	diff
	continued

---

diff3 [*options*] *file1 file2 file3*

Compare three files and report the differences with the following codes:

    ==   all three files differ.
    ==1   *file1* is different.
    ==2   *file2* is different.
    ==3   *file3* is different.

options

    -e   create an editor script to incorporate into *file1* differences between *file2* and *file3*.
    -x   create an editor script to incorporate into *file1* differences between all three files.
    -3   create an editor script to incorporate into *file1* differences between *file1* and *file3*.

diff3

---

diffmk *file1 file2 markedfile*

Compare *file1* with *file2* and create a third file *markedfile*, which consists of the text of *file2* and "change mark" (**.mc**) commands which will print change bars showing the differences between *file1* and *file2* when *markedfile* is formatted with **nroff** or **troff**.

diffmk

---

dircmp *dir1 dir2*

Compare the contents of *dir1* and *dir2*.

options

    -d   execute **diff** on the files which differ.
    -s   suppress identical file messages.
    -w*n* change the output line length to *n*.

dircmp

---

dirname	**dirname** *pathname*
	Print *pathname* excluding last level. Used to strip the actual filename from a pathname. See **basename**.

dis	**dis** [*options*] *files*
	Disassemble the object or archive *files*.
	options
	-d *section*
	limit the disassembly to specified *section*, printing the offset of the data.
	-da *section*
	limit the disassembly to specified *section*, printing the actual address of the data.
	-F *function*
	limit the disassembly to *function*.
	-l *string*
	limit the disassembly to the library file *string*. For example, *string* would be "x" for **libx.a**.
	-L invokes a lookup of C source labels.
	-o print octal output.
	-t *section*
	limit the disassembly to *section* and produce text output.
	-V print the version number of the disassembler.

disable	**disable** [*options*] *printer*
	Deactivate *printer*, so that **lp** requests do not print.
	options
	-c cancel requests that are currently printing on *printer*.
	-r["*reason*"]
	associate a *reason* with the deactivation of *printer*. *reason* is reported by **lpstat** and has a default value when *reason* or **-r** is not specified.

du [*options*] [*directories*]   **du**

Print the number of blocks used by each subdirectory in named directory or directories. The current directory is the default.

options

-a   produce an entry for each file in each named directory.
-s*dir*   give only the grand total for each named directory *dir*.

---

dump [*options*][*modifiers*] *objfiles*   **dump**

Produce output from selected parts of *objfiles*.

options

-a   produce the header of each archive.
-c   produce the string table.
-f   produce header for *objfiles*.
-g   produce the global symbol for an archive.
-h   produce the section headers.
-l   produce the line information.
-o   produce optional headers.
-r   produce the relocation information.
-s   produce the sections.
-t   produce the symbol tables.
-z *name*
       produce the line numbers for *name*.

modifiers

-d *num*
       start dump at section *num*.
+d *num*
       end dump at section *num*
-n *name*
       produce information for *name* only.
-p   do not produce header information.
-t *index*
       produce the indexed table entry starting at *index*.
+t *index*
       produce the indexed table entry ending at *index*.

dump
continued
	-u underline filenames.
	-v produce a symbolic dump.
	-z *name,num*
	        produce line number entries for *name* starting at *num*.
	+z *num*
	        produce line number entries ending at *num*

echo	**echo** [*string*] Copy *string* to the standard output. If *string* not specified, echo a newline. See Section 2 for more information on **echo**.

ed	**ed** [*options*] [*file*]
	
	The standard text editor. If the named *file* does not exist, **ed** will create it; otherwise the existing named *file* will be opened for editing.
	options
	    -s suppress character counts, diagnostics, and "!" prompt.
	    -p *string*
	        user defined prompt string.
	    -x read a file encrypted with **crypt**.

edit	**edit** [**-r**] [**file**] A line-oriented text editor. **-r** recover file after system crash

efl	**efl** [*options*] [*files*]
	
	Convert a file from EFL (Extended FORTRAN Language) to FORTRAN. Used as a preprocessor for **f77**.
	    -C include comments in the generated program (default).
	    -w suppress warning messages.
	    -# suppress comments in the generated program. Convert a file from EFL to FORTRAN.

egrep [*options*] [*regexp*] [*files*]   **egrep**

Search one or more *files* for lines that match a full regular expression *regexp*. Regular expressions are described in Section 3. See also **grep** and **fgrep**.

options

-**f** *file* take pattern from *file*.
-**v**   print all non-matching lines.

There may be additional machine-specific options.

---

enable [*printer*]   **enable**

Enable the lp printer *printer*. See also **disable** and **lpstat**.

---

enroll   **enroll**

Enter the protected mail system. **enroll** prompts for a password. See also **xsend** and **xget**.

---

env [-] [*variable=value* ...] [*command*]   **env**

Modify the current environment with variables redefined as specified and execute *command* in modified environment. If *command* is not specified, only the modified environment is printed.

option

-       ignore current environment entirely.

---

eqn [*options*] [*files*]   **eqn**

Numerical equation preprocessor for **troff**. See Section 7 for more information on **eqn**.

options

-**d***xy* use *x* and *y* as start and stop delimiters.
-**f***n*   change to font *n*.
-**p***n*   reduce the superscript size by *n* points.
-**s***n*   reduce the point size by *n* points.

---

ex

ex [*options*] *files*

A line-oriented text editor — a superset of **ed** and the root of **vi**. See Section 4 for more information on **vi** and **ex**.

options

-     suppress all warning, interactive, and error messages.
- **-r** *file* recover *file* after an editor or system crash.
- **-R**   set **read-only** mode to prevent accidental file overwrite.
- **-t** *tag* edit the file containing *tag* and position the editor at its definition.
- **-v**   invoke **vi**.
- **-x**   create or edit an encrypted file.
- **+** *cmd* Edit by an editor search or positioning command *cmd*.

expr

expr *arguments*

Evaluate the named *arguments* as expressions and print the result. Expression elements and operators must be separated by spaces.

arguments

expr1 | *expr2*
> True if either expression *expr1* or *expr2* is true.

expr1 & *expr2*
> True if expression *expr1* or *expr2* are both true.

expr1 {*op*} *expr2*
> yield 1 if the indicated comparison is true, 0 if false. *op* is one of the following: =, , =, , =, !=.

expr1 + *expr2*
> add the expressions.

expr1 - *expr2*
> subtract the expressions.

expr1 * *expr2*
> multiply the expressions.

expr1 / *expr2*
> divide the expressions.

expr1 % *expr2*
: take the remainder after division of the arguments.

expr1 : *expr2*
: compare *expr1* with *expr2*.
: *expr2* must be regular.

(*expr*) evaluate expressions enclosed in parentheses first. (Expressions are normally evaluated left to right.)

The characters &, |, and * must be escaped (preceded with \).

expr
continued

---

f77 [*options*] *files*

The UNIX FORTRAN 77 compiler.

options

-1
: compile DO loops.

-66
: do not extend for **f66** compatibility.

-c
: suppress loading and produce **.o** files.

-C
: produce code for range-checking.

-E *string*
: use *string* as EFL option.

-f
: use the floating point processor.

-F
: invoke EFL and RATFOR preprocessor and place the result in *file*.**f**.

-g
: produce additional symbol table information.

-m
: invoke **m4** preprocessor to RATFOR or EFL file.

-N *flag* *n*
: establish the maximum size of various dynamically allocated compiler internal data structures.

    flag is one of:

    c - number of looping structures
    l - number of labels
    n - number of identifiers
    q - number of equivalences
    s - number of statement numbers
    x - number of external names

-o *outfile*
: send output to *outfile*.

f77

☞

---

f77
continued
	-O invoke object code optimizer.
	-onetrip
	      compile DO loops.
	-p set up object files for profiling.
	-R *string*
	      use *string* as RATFOR option.
	-S produce assembler **.s** files.
	-u variable type undefined.
	-U do not convert upper case letters to lower case.
	-v print compilation progress report.
	-w suppress warning messages.

factor	**factor** [*num*] Produce *num*'s prime factors or prompt for input.
false	**false** Return an unsuccessful exit status. Normally used under the **sh** command. See also **true**.

fgrep	**fgrep** [*options*] [*pattern*] [*files*]
	
	Search one or more *files* for lines that match a fixed-string *pattern*. **fgrep** does not support regular expressions. See also **egrep** and **grep**.
	
	options
	    -b precede each line with block number.
	    -c print only count of matched lines.
	    -e *pattern*
	        this option is for *pattern* which begins with "-".
	    -f*file* take pattern from *file*.
	    -l list only filenames.
	    -n precede each line with line number.
	    -v print only non-matching lines.
	    -x print only lines that match exactly.

file [*option*] *files*   **file**

Classify the named *files*, according to the type of data
they contain. **file** checks the magic file (usually
/etc/magic) to identify files containing a numeric or
string constant indicating its type.

options

    -c   check only the magic file for format errors.

    -f *file* take the names of files to be examined
                from *file*.

    -m *file*
          use *file* as the magic file.

---

find *pathnames condition(s)*   **find**

Search one or more *pathnames* for files that meet the
specified *conditions*. At least one *pathname* and one
condition must be specified. Conditions may be
grouped using escaped parentheses (\(and \)), negated
with !, or given as alternatives by separating them with
-o. If you want the results of the search to be
displayed, be sure to use the **-print** option.

condition

    -name *name*
          only files which match the specified *name*.
          Shell metacharacters may be used, but
          should be escaped or quoted.

    -perm *onum*
          only files with file permission flags exactly
          matching the octal number *onum*.

    -type *c*
          only files whose type is *c*. *c* may be **b**
          (block special file), **c** (character special
          file), **d** (directory), **p** (fifo or named pipe),
          or **f** (plain file).

    -links *n*
          only files with *n* links.

    -user *uname*
          only files belonging to the user *uname*.
          uname may be a user name or a *uid* num-
          ber.

☞

---

find
continued

-group *gname*
> only files belonging to the group *gname*. *gname* may be a user name or a *gid* number.

-size *n*[c]
> only files which are *n* blocks long, or if **c** is specified, *n* characters long.

-atime [+,-]*n*
> only files that have been accessed in more than (+*n*), less than (-*n*), or exactly *n* days.

-mtime [+,-]*n*
> only files which have been modified in more than (+*n*), less than (-*n*), or exactly *n* days.

-ctime [+,-]*n*
> only files which have been changed in more than (+*n*), less than (-*n*), or exactly *n* days.

-exec *cmd* {}\;
> only files which return a zero value as exit status when *cmd* is executed. Within the command, the argument {} is replaced with the current pathname. The entire sequence must be followed with an escaped semicolon (\;).

-ok *cmd* {}\;
> same as **-exec**, except that user is prompted before executing.

-print causes the pathname of each selected file to be printed.

-cpio *dev*
> write files on *dev* with **cpio**.

-newer *file*
> only files which have been modified more recently than *file*.

-depth
> operate on a parent directory after any subdirectories it contains. Useful when using **find** with **cpio**.

fsplit [*options*] *files*

Split a FORTRAN file into program segments if possible.

options

-e	input is in EFL format.
-f	input is in F77 format (the default).
-r	input is in RATFOR format.
-s	force all lines to 72 or fewer characters with trailing blanks removed.

---

ged [*options*] [*GPS file* . . .]

Invoke interactive graphical editor. This accesses additional commands with which to display, construct or edit files on TEKTRONIX 4010 series display terminals. *GPS file* is a file containing three graphical objects: *lines*, *arc*, and *text*.

options

-e	do not erase the screen before initial display.
-r*n*	display region number *n*.
-R	restricted shell invoked on use of !.
-u	display the entire GPS "universe," or Cartesian plane.

---

get [*options*] *files*

Retrieve a particular version of an SCCS *file* and print its version number and total number of lines. See Section 9 for more information on SCCS.

options

-a*n*	retrieve delta sequence number *n*.
-b	create new branch.
-c*date*	ignore changes made after *date* (format yy[mm[dd[hh[mm[ss]]]]]).
-e	retrieve for editing.
-g	suppress version retrieval.
-i*list*	include a *list* of changes.
-k	do not replace id keywords.

☞

get
continued
	-l[p]*file*
	    write delta summary to *file*. -lp displays a
	    summary.
	-m precede each line with sid version number.
	-n precede each line with %M% keyword.
	-p write retrieved text to standard output.
	-r*sid* retrieve version number *sid*.
	-s suppress normal output.
	-t retrieve latest version of a release.
	-w*string*
	    substitute *string* for %W%.
	-x*list* exclude the *list* of deltas.

---

getopt

set — 'getopt *string* $*'

Parse command options for shell procedures.

   string a string of option letters.

---

getopts

getopts *string name* [*arg*]

Parse positional parameters and check for legal options. Should be used in place of **getopt** in shell procedures.

string must contain the option letters that the command using **getopts** will recognize. The next option is placed in the shell variable *name*. If an option is followed by a colon, the option must be followed by one or more arguments.

---

glossary

glossary [*term*]

Print the definition of *term*. If *term* is not specified, a selection menu is printed.

---

graph

graph [*options*]

Draw a graph, using pairs of numbers taken from standard input as x-y coordinates. The graph may be printed using **plot**. See also **spline**.

options

graph
continued

-a *spacing* [*start*]
  provide abscissas with *spacing* (default 1) and starting point *start* (default 0).

-b   break after each input.

-c *string*
  label each point with *string*.

-g *n*   grid style: 0=no grid, 1=tick grid, 2=full grid.

-h *n*   space *n* height.

-l *label*
  use *label* for the graph.

-m *n*   connecting lines style: 0=disconnected, 1=connected.

-r *n*   move fraction *n* right before plotting.

-s   save screen.

-t   transpose axes.

-u *n*   move fraction *n* up before plotting.

-w *n*   space *n* height.

-x [l] *lower upper spacing*
  manual x-axis layout. The optional l gives a logarithmic axis.

-y [l] *lower upper spacing*
  manual y-axis layout. The optional l gives a logarithmic axis.

---

graphics [*options*]

graphics

Enable graphics path and change the shell prompt.

options

  -r   access is created in a restricted environment. The restricted shell, *rsh*, is invoked.

---

greek [*option*]

greek

A terminal filter that reinterprets the extended character set of a 128-character TELETYPE® Model 37 terminal for other terminals.

option

  -T *term*
    use terminal type *term*.

grep	**grep** [*options*] *regexp* [*files*]
	Search through one or more *files* for a regular expression *regexp*. Regular expressions are described in Section 3. See also **egrep** and **fgrep**.
	options
	-b precede each line with its block number.
	-c print only a count of matched lines.
	-i ignore upper/lower case distinctions.
	-l print only the names of files containing matching lines.
	-n precede each line with its line number in the file.
	-s suppress error messages for nonexistent or unreadable files.
	-v print all lines that do not match.
help	**help** [*command*] [*error*]
	Give an explanation of a *command* or an *error* message number.
helpadm	**helpadm**
	Entry to the administrator's help database management menus.
hp	**hp** [*options*]
	Support Hewlett-Packard terminals for *ditroff* output.
	options
	-e terminal with display enhancements.
	-m remove newlines from output.
hpio	**hpio** *options* [*flags*]
	Tape file archiver for tape cartridges in Hewlett-Packard 2645A terminals. The two options have different flags, as follows:
	hpio -o[rc] *file*
	Copy out a file onto the tape drive.

hpio -i[rt] [-n *count***]**

Copy in files from the tape drive.

flags

- **a**   ask before bringing in a file.
- **c**   include a checksum at the end of *file*.
- **r**   use the right tape drive (left drive used by default).
- **t**   print a table of contents only. No files are created.
- **-n** *count*

  bring in the number of files specified by *count*. Omit the **-n** option to bring in 1 file (default) or specify an arbitrarily large *count* to bring in all files.

hpio
continued

---

hyphen *files*

List all hyphenated words contained in one or more *files*.

hyphen

---

id

List user and group ids and corresponding processes.

id

---

init

init spawns processes on terminals by reading the **/etc/inittab** file.

init

---

install [*options***]** *file* **[***dir***]**

Used primarily in *makefiles* to update files. Old versions of *file* in one of the default or user-supplied directories are overwritten.

- **-c** *dir*   replace *file* in *dir* only if another version of *file* is not already present in *dir*.
- **-f** *dir*   force *file* to be copied into *dir*.
- **-i**   ignore the default directories. Use only the supplied directories to search for *file*.
- **-n** *dir*   if *file* is not found in any of the default directories, place it in *dir*.

install

☞

install *continued*	**-o** save the old version of *file* in **OLD***file* rather than overwriting it. **-s** suppress all messages except error messages.

ipcrm

ipcrm [*options*]

Remove a message queue, semaphore set, or shared memory identifier as specified by the *options*.

options

    -m *shmid*
        remove *shmid*, shared memory identifier.
    -q *msqid*
        remove *msqid*, message queue identifier.
    -s *semid*
        remove *semid*, semaphore identifier.
    -M *shmkey*
        remove the *shmid* created with key *shmkey* from the system.
    -Q *msgkey*
        remove the *msqid* created with key *msgkey* from the system.
    -S *semkey*
        remove the *semid* created with key *semkey* and its associated data structure from the system.

ipcs

ipcs [*options*]

Print information about active inter-process communication facilities.

options

    -m   report on active shared memory segments.
    -q   report on active message queues.
    -s   report on active semaphores.

With the **-m**, **-q**, or **-s** options, only the specified inter-process facility is reported on. Otherwise information about all three is printed.

    -a   use all of the print options.
    -b   report the largest allowable size information.

-c	report the creator's login name and group.	**ipcs** *continued*
-o	report on outstanding usage.	
-p	report the process number information.	
-t	report the time information.	

-C_file_ use *file* to store core rather than /dev/kmem.

-N_namelist_

     use the argument for *namelist* in place of the default (/**unix**).

---

ismpx [-s]

ismpx

Report whether standard input is running under **layers**. Useful for shell scripts that send programs to a windowing terminal or depend on screen size.

option

  -s print nothing; return proper exit status.

---

join [*options*] *file1 file2*

join

Join the common lines of sorted *file1* and sorted *file2*. The output contains the common field and the remainder of each line from *file1* and *file2*.

option

  -a_n_ list unpairable lines in file n (n is 1 or 2).

  -e *s* replace empty output fields with *s*.

  -j_n m_ join on the *m*th field of file n. If n is not specified, use both files.

  -o *n.m* output line has the fields specified by n, a file number, and m, a field number. The common field is not printed unless requested.

  -t_c_ use character c as a field separator (tab) for both input and output. Every appearance of c in a line is significant.

---

jterm

jterm

Reset layer of windowing terminal after a program changes the terminal attributes of the layer. Used only under **layers**.

---

jwin	**jwin**
	Print size of layer. Used only under **layers**.
kill	**kill** [*-signal*] *pid*
	Terminate a process. You must be either the owner of the process or a superuser.
	-signal the signal number or name. With a signal number of 9, the kill is absolute.
	pid the process id number (obtained from **ps**). Using the C Shell, you can kill using job specifiers as well as *pids*.
layers	**layers** [*options*]
	A layer multiplexer for windowing terminals. **layers** manages asynchronous windows on a windowing terminal.
	options
	-d print sizes of the text, data, and *bss* portions of a downloaded firmware patch on standard error.
	-f *file* initialize **layers** with a configuration specified by *file*. Each line of *file* is a layer to be created and has the following format:
	origin *x* origin *y* corner *x* corner *y* *commands*
	-p print the downloading protocol statistics and a trace of a downloaded firmware patch on standard error.
	-s report protocol statistics on standard error after exiting **layers**.
	-t turn on **xt** driver packet tracing and produce a trace dump on standard error after exiting **layers**.
	layers_prgm a file containing a firmware patch that **layers** downloads to the terminal. Downloading occurs before layers are created or *commands* are executed.

ld [*options*] *objfiles*   **ld**

Combine several *objfiles*, in the specified order, into a
single executable object module (**a.out**).

options

-a   create an absolute, executable file.

-e *name*
        name of entry point (default is location 0).

-f *fill*   set the hole filler pattern to *fill*.

-l *x*   search   the   library   **/lib/lib***x***.a**   and
        /usr/lib/lib*x***.a** (the placement of this option
        on the line is significant).

-L *dir* search the directory *dir* for library files

-m   produce a primitive load map.

-M   print messages when multiply-defined ex-
        ternal definitions are found.

-N   put the data section immediately after the
        text section.

-o *file* send the output to *file* (default is **a.out**).

-r   allow output to be subject to another **ld**.

-s   remove symbol table and relocation bits.

-t   suppress "multiply-defined symbols" error
        messages.

-u *symbol*
        enter *symbol* in symbol table.

-V   print the version of **ld**.

-VS *num*
        place the version number *num* in the
        header of the output file.

-x   enter only external and static symbols in
        output.

-z   suppress binding to address 0.

---

lex [*options*] [*files*]   **lex**

Generate lexical analysis programs from the input regular expressions and C/RATFOR program actions.

options

-c   program actions are in C {default}.

-n   suppress the output summary.

-r   program actions are in RATFOR.

-t   write lex.yy.c program to standard output.

---

lex *continued*	**-v** summary of machine-generated statistics.

line

line

Read the next line from standard input and write it to standard output.

lint

lint [*options*] *files*

Detect bugs, portability problems, and other possible errors in the specified C programs. By default, function definitions are defined in the **llib-lc.ln** library.

options

    -a   ignore long values assigned to variables that are not long.

    -b   ignore break statements that cannot be reached.

    -c   do not execute the second pass of **lint**.

    -D   same as **-D** of **cc**.

    -h   do not test for bugs, style, and extraneous information.

    -I   same as **-I** of *cc*

    -l*x*   use library **llib-l***x***.ln** in addition to **llib-lc.ln**.

    -n   do not check for compatibility.

    -o *lib*   create a lint library **llib-l.***lib***.ln** from the output of the first pass of **lint**.

    -p   check for portability.

    -u   ignore undefined functions and variables.

    -U*name*

        remove any initial definition of *name*.

    -v   ignore unused arguments within functions.

    -x   ignore unused variables referred to by external declarations.

list

list [*options*] *source . . . object*

Produce listing of C source and object code with line numbers.

options

    -F*function*

        limit the listing to the function *function*.

-h	do no print heading information.	**list**
-V	print the version number of *list*.	*continued*

ln [*option*] *file* [*file2* ...] *target* **ln**

Create a pseudonym (link) for *file* named *target* or link the specified files to *target* when the specified *target* is an existing directory.

option

   -f   force the link to occur without questions.

---

locate [*keyword* ...] **locate**

Provide a list of commands associated with *keyword*.

---

login [*user*] **login**

Sign on and identify yourself to the system. At the beginning of each terminal session, the system prompts you for your *user* name and, if relevant, a password.

---

logname **logname**

Print the value of the $LOGNAME environment variable located in /etc/profile.

---

lorder *objfiles* **lorder**

List pairs of object file names. The **lorder** output can be sent to **tsort** to create a random library.

---

lp [*options*] *files* **lp**

Print the *files* with the specified options.

options

   -c   copy the files to the print spooler so that changes that occur to *file* after the *lp* command do not effect the printout.

   -d *dest* send the output to the printer *dest*.

☞

lp
continued
	-m send mail upon completion.
	-n *number*
	        specify the *number* of copies to print.
	-o *option*
	        set the printer specific *option*.
	-s suppress messages.
	-t *title* use *title* for the printout.
	-w confirm the printing with a message on the user's terminal.

---

lpstat

lpstat [*options*]

Print the **lp** print queue status. The *list* can be a comma separated list of printers or printer classes enclosed in double quotes (").

-a[*list*]
> report whether the printer *list* is accepting requests.

-c[*list*]
> report information about printer classes.

-d   report the default destination.

-o[*list*]
> report on the output request. *list* can contain request ids.

-p *list* report on the status of the printers.

-r   report on the scheduler.

-s   summarize the print status.

-t   report all status information.

-u[*list*]
> report the status for the *list* of users. *list* contains login names.

-v[*list*]
> report the status of each printer and the pathname of the device associated with it.

---

ls

ls [*options*] [*directory*]

List the files contained in the current or specified *directory*.

options

    -a   list all files including "." files.
    -b   show non-printing characters in octal.

-c	list by file creation/modification time.	**ls**
-C	list multicolumn output to a file or pipe.	*continued*

-c list by file creation/modification time.
-C list multicolumn output to a file or pipe.
-d list only directory name, not its contents.
-f interpret each argument as a directory.
-F append "/" to directories and "*" to executable files.
-g suppress group id from long listing.
-i list the i-node for each file.
-l long format listing.
-m force stream output format.
-n use the GID and UID number rather than owner and group names in the long listing.
-o suppress owner id from the long listing.
-p append "/" to directories.
-q show non-printing characters as "?".
-r list in reverse order.
-R recursively list subdirectories as well as current directory.
-s print size of the files in blocks.
-t list files according to the file modification dates.
-u list files according to the file access time.
-x list the files across the page.

---

m4 *[options]* *[files]*   **m4**

Macro processor for RATFOR, C, and other programs.

options

-B*n* set push-back argument collection buffers to *n* (default is 4,096).

-D*name*[*=value*]
define *name* to *value* or null if *value* is not specified.

-e operate interactively.

-H*n* set symbol table hash array to *n*.

-s enable line sync output.

-S*n* set call stack size to *n* (default is 100 slots).

-T*n* set token buffer size to *n* (default is 512 bytes).

-U*name*
undefine *name*.

mail

mail [*options*] [*users*]

Read mail and send mail to other *users*. Use "?" for a summary of commands.

options for sending mail

- **-o**   suppress the address optimization facility.
- **-s**   suppress the addition of a newline at the top of the message being sent.
- **-w**   force mail to be sent to remote users without waiting for remote transfer program to be completed.
- **-t**   print a "To:" line at the heading of the letter, showing the names of the recipients.

options for reading mail:

- **-e**   do not print mail. Exit with status 0 if mail exists, otherwise exit with status 1.
- **-f** *file* use *file* for the mail message.
- **-h**   a window of messages is displayed rather than the latest message.
- **-p**   print all messages without pausing.
- **-q**   terminate on an interrupt.
- **-r**   print oldest messages first.
- **-F** *names*
  forward all incoming mail to *names*.

mailx

mailx [*options*] [*users*]

Read mail with "command mode" features available, or send mail to other *users*. Use "**help**" for a summary of commands.

options

- **-e**   exit with status 0 if mail exists, otherwise exit with status 1.
- **-f***file* read *file* for mail messages.
- **-F**   place a copy of the mail in a special file named for the first person to receive the mail.
- **-h***n*   software flag: specify number of network connections ("hops") made so far to be *n*.
- **-H**   print header information.
- **-i**   ignore interrupts.

-n	do not read the **Mail.rc** file.	**mailx** *continued*
-N	do not print header information.	

-r *address*
    use *address* for the network destination.

-s *subject*
    specify *subject*.

-u *user*
    read *user*'s mail.

-U   use internet and not **uucp** addresses.

---

make [*options*] [*targets*]
                                                          make

Update one or more targets according to the list of dependencies located in a file called **makefile** or **Makefile** in the current directory. See Section 9 for more information on **make**.

options

-b	compatibility mode for old versions of *makefile*.
-d	print detailed debugging information.
-e	override *makefile* assignments with environment variables.

-f *makefile*
    take *makefile* as the description file; a filename of "-" denotes standard input.

-i	ignore command error codes (or .IGNORE).
-k	abandon work on current entry; continue with unrelated entries.
-m	print a memory map.
-n	print commands, but do not execute.
-p	print macro definitions and *makefile* descriptions.
-q	return 0 if file is up to date.
-r	do not use "default" rules.
-s	do not print command lines (.SILENT in description file).
-t	touch the target files, causing them to be updated.

makekey

makekey

Create a "good" encryption key.

man

man [*options*] [*section*] *command*

Print the page in the *UNIX Programmer's Manual* that describes *command*. *command* is assumed to be described in Section 1 unless you specify an optional *section* from 1 to 8.

options

- **-12**   print output in 12 pitch.
- **-c**   invoke **col**.
- **-d**   search current directory rather than **/usr/man**.
- **-k** *keyword*
  print manual section containing *keyword*.
- **-T** [*tty*]
  format pages for device *tty* (default is 450).
- **-w**   print only pathname of manual page.
- **-y**   use non-compacted macro version.

mesg

mesg [*options*]

Print the current state of write permission on your terminal. The permission is changed with the specified *options*.

options

- **n**   forbid **write** messages.
- **y**   allow **write** messages.

mkdir

mkdir *directories*

Create one or more *directories*. You must have write permission in the parent directory in order to create a directory.

mknod

mknod *name type major minor*

Build a special file for a device.

name	**mknod**
name of the special file crated.	*continued*

type

c	character-type device.
b	block-type device.
p	named pipe device.

major

major device number.

minor

minor device number.

Options are system-specific.

---

mm [*options*] [*files*]

Format one or more *files* with **nroff** using the memo-randum **macro** (**mm**) package. See Section 6 for more information on the **mm** package.

options

-c	invoke **col**.
-E	invoke -e option of **nroff**.
-t	invoke **tbl**.
-T*tty*	type of output terminal is *tty*.
-y	use non-compacted version of **mm**.

mm

---

mmt

Like **mm**, but uses **troff**.

mmt

---

mount [*special*] [*dir*]

Report the status of mounted special files. When this command is issued with *special* device and *dir* argu-ments, the *special* device is mounted on *dir*. **umount** *special* unmounts a special device.

Options are system-specific.

mount

---

mv [*options*] *file target*

Move (or rename) *file* to *target*, or move one or more *files* to the existing directory *target*.

mv

☞

---

mv
continued

options

-     all arguments which follow are file (or directory) names. This includes names beginning with "-".
- **-f**   force mode, suppress error messages.
- **-i**   request interactive confirmation of each move.

---

newform

newform [*options*] *files*

Filter *files* with the options specified.

options

-a[*n*]   append the correct number of characters to the end of the line so that it has the correct *line length* (-l). When *n* is specified *n* characters are appended.

-b   remove characters from the front of the lines until each line is the correct line length (-l).

-c*m*   let *m* be the prefix/append character (the default is a space).

-e   remove characters from the end of the lines until each line is the correct line length (-l).

-f   print the tab character on standard output.

-i*tabspec*
    convert tabs to *tabspec* (*tabspec* default is 8 spaces). See **tabs** for *tabspec* format.

-l*n*   use *n* for the line length. The default line length is 80 characters when the -l option is not specified.

-o*tabspec*
    convert *tabspec* to tabs (*tabspec* default is 8 spaces). See **tabs** for *tabspec* format.

-p[*n*]   prefix the correct number of characters to the end of the line so that it has the correct *line length* (-l). When *n* is specified, *n* characters are appended.

-s   move all leading characters up to the first tab to the end of the line.

newgrp [*group*]　　　　　　　　　　　　　　**newgrp**

Login to *group*. If *group* name is not specified, your
original group is reinstated.

---

news [*options*] [*items*]　　　　　　　　　　　**news**

Consult the directory **/usr/news** (default) for information on current events.

options

-a   print all items regardless of currency.
-n   print the names of the news items but not
       their contents.
-s   report the number of current news items.

items

refers to particular news items to be printed.

---

nice [*options*] *command* [*arguments*]　　　　　**nice**

Execute a *command* and *arguments* with low priority.

options

-*n*   (Bourne shell only.) Run *command* with a
       niceness of *n* (1-19). The higher the nice-
       ness number, the lower the priority. {De-
       fault = 4}

-*n*   (C shell only.) Run *command* with a nice-
       ness of negative *n*. This raises the priority.
       Only the superuser may do this.

+*n*   (C Shell only.) Run *command* with a nice-
       ness of *n*. This lowers the priority.

−−*n* (Bourne Shell only.) Run *command* with a
       niceness of negative *n*. This raises the pri-
       ority. Only the superuser may do this.

---

nl [*options*] [*file*]　　　　　　　　　　　　　**nl**

Number the lines of a *file* in logical page segments. At
the start of each page, numbering is reset to 1.

options

-b*type*

      number lines according to *type*. Values
      are:

nl
continued

          a all lines.
          n no lines.
          t text lines only.

-dxx use xx as the logical page delimiter characters (default is ":").

-f$type$ number according to $type$ and omit the footer. Values are as in **-b** above.

-h$type$
        number lines according to $type$. Values are as in **-b** above.

-in increment each line number by n (default is 1).

-ln interpret n blank lines as 1.

-n$format$
        set line number format. Values are:
        ln left justify, omit leading zeroes.
        rn right justify, omit leading zeroes (the default).
        rz right justify.

-p   do not reset numbering at start of pages.

-sc separate line number with character c.

-vn start numbering each page with n (default is 1).

-wn set line number digits to n (default is 6).

nm

nm [*options*] [*objfiles*]

Print the symbol table in alphabetical order for one or more object files.

options

    -e   report only external and static symbols.
    -f   report all information.
    -h   suppress the header.
    -n   sort the external symbols
    -o   report values in octal.
    -p   precede each symbol with its type key (used for parsing).
    -r   report the name of the output file on each line.
    -u   report only the undefined symbols.
    -v   sort the external symbols.
    -x   report values in hexadecimal.

symbol values

A	absolute symbol.
C	common symbol.
D	data segment symbol.
F	file symbol.
T	text segment symbol.

nm
continued

---

nohup *command* [*arguments*] **&**

Continue to execute the named *command* and optional command *arguments* after you log out (make command immune to hangups).

nohup

---

nroff [*options*] [*files*]

Format one or more text *files* for printing. See Section 5 for more information on **nroff**.

options

-c *name*
>prepend /usr/lib/macros/cmp.[nt].[dt].*name* to files.

-e space words equally.

-h use tabs in large spaces.

-i read standard input after files are processed.

-k *name*
>compact macros and output to [dt].*name*.

-m *name*
>prepend **/usr/lib/tmac/tmac.***name* to files.

-n *n* number first page *n*.

-o *list* print only pages contained in *list*. A page range is specified by *n-m*.

-q invoke simultaneous input-output of **.rd** requests.

-r *an* set register *a* to *n*.

-s *n* stop every *n* pages.

-T *name*
>output is for device type *name*.

-u *n* embolden characters by overstriking *n* times.

-z do not print standard output; only print error messages such as those from a **.tm** (terminal message) request.

nroff

---

od	**od** [*options*] [*file*] [[+] [*offset*[.][**b**]]]
	Produce an octal dump of the named *file*.
	options
	-b display bytes as octal.
	-c display bytes as ASCII.
	-d display words as decimal.
	-o display words as octal (the default).
	-s display 16-bit words as signed decimal.
	-x display words as hexadecimal.
	+ required if *file* not specified.
	offset
	start dumping *file* at octal offset.
	. decimal offset.
	b offset in 512-byte blocks.

pack	**pack** [*option*] *files*
	Compact each *file* and place the result in *file*.**z**. The original file is replaced. To restore packed *files* to their original form, see **pcat** and **unpack**.
	options
	- print number of times each byte is used, relative frequency, and byte code.
	-f force the **pack**.

passwd	**passwd** *user*
	Create or change a password associated with a *user* name. Only the owner or superuser may change a password.

paste	**paste** [*options*] *files*
	Merge corresponding lines of one or more *files*, horizontally. Columns are separated by a tab character.
	options
	-s merge subsequent lines from one file.
	- replaces a file name with the standard input.

-d *char*
>   replace newline characters with *char*. Values for *char* are:

n	newline.
****	backslash.
t	tab.
0	empty string.

---

pcat *files*

Display (as with **cat**) one or more packed *files*. See also **pack** and **unpack**.

---

pg [*options*] [*files*]

Display the named *files* on a terminal, one page at a time. After each screen is displayed, you are prompted to display the next page by pressing the RETURN key.

options

-c	overwrite lines.
-e	do not pause between files.
-f	do not split long lines.
-n	issue a **pg** command only (no carriage return) to perform the command.

-p *string*
>   use *string* for the command prompt.

-s	display messages in standout (reverse video) mode.

-number
+linenumber
>   begin displaying two lines before *linenumber*.

+/pattern/
>   begin displaying two lines before *pattern*.

---

pic [*option*] [*files*] `

A preprocessor for *nroff* and *troff* that formats graphics commands contained in *files* and enclosed by **.PS** and **.PE** requests. See Section 7 for more information on **pic**.

---

pr

pr [*options*] [*files*]

Format one or more *files* according to *options* to standard output. Each page includes a heading that consists of the page number, filename, date, and time.

options

-**a**   multi-column format.
-**d**   double-spaced format.
-**e** *cn*   set input tabs to every *n*th position and use *c* as field delimiter (defaults are *n*=8 and *c*=tab).
-**f**   use form feed (^L) character instead of a series of newlines to separate pages.
-**h** *string*
  replace default header with *string*.
-**i** *cn*   for output, replace white space with field delimiter *c* every *n*th position (defaults are *n*=8 and *c*=tab).
-**l***n*   set page length to *n* (default is 66).
-**m**   merge the files and print them, one file in each column (overrides -*n* and -**a**).
+*n*   begin printing at page *n* (default is 1).
-*n*   produce output with *n*-columns (default is 1).
-**n** *cn*   number lines with numbers *n* digits in length, followed by field separator *c* (defaults are *n*=5 and *c*=tab).
-**o***n*   offset each line *n* spaces (default is 0).
-**p**   pause before each page.
-**r**   do not print messages on failure to open files.
-**s***c*   separate columns with *c* (default is a tab).
-**t**   omit the page header and trailer.
-**w***n*   set line width to *n* (default is 72 for equal width multicolumn output).

prof

prof [*options*] [*file*]

Display the profile data for *file*. Choose only one of the sort options -**a** -**c** -**n** -**t**.

options

-**a**   list output by symbol address.

-c	list output by decreasing number of calls.	**prof** *continued*
-g	output non-global symbols.	
-h	do not output the report heading.	

-m *mondata*
  use *mondata* as the input profile file.

-n	list by symbol name.
-o	output addresses in octal. This option cannot be used with the **-x** option.
-s	produce a summary for standard output.
-t	list output by decreasing total time percentage.
-x	output addresses in hexadecimal. This option cannot be used with the **-o** option.
-z	include zero usage calls.

---

prs [*options*] *files*

Print all or portions of one or more SCCS *files*. See
Section 9 for more information on SCCS.

options

-a	print information for removed deltas.

-c [*yy*[*mm*[*dd*[*hh*[*mm*[*ss*]]]]]]
  delta cutoff date.

-d [*keywords*]
  specify data output with SCCS *keywords*.
  See Section 9 for available *keywords*.

-e	include deltas from earlier than the -r*sid* specified option.
-l	include deltas from later than the -r*sid* specified option

-r [*sid*]
  print the SCCS id version number *sid*.

prs

---

ps [*options*]

Report on active processes.

options

-a	all processes except group leaders and processes not associated with a terminal.

-c*file* use *file* for core image (default is
  /dev/mem or **/dev/kmem**).

ps

☞

---

ps *continued*	**-d** all processes except group leaders. **-e** all processes. **-f** generate a full listing. **-g** *list* restrict listing to processes associated with the comma-separated groups in *list*. **-l** long listing. **-n** *name* use the alternate namelist *name* (default is **/unix**). **-p** *list* only processes associated with process ids in the comma-separated *list*. **-s** *dev* use *dev* for swap device (default is **/dev/swap**). **-t** *list* only processes associated with terminals in the comma-separated *list*. **-u** *list* only processes associated with users in the comma-separated *list*.

ptx	**ptx** [*options*] [*file1* [*file2*]]
	
	Generate a permuted index of *file1* into *file2*. Files must be formatted with **nroff -mptx** to actually produce the index. If files are not specified, standard input and output are used.
	
	options
	   -b *file* use characters in *file* to separate words.
	   -f sort with no upper/lower case distinction.
	   -g *n* change the space between columns to *n* (default is 3).
	   -i *file* ignore the keywords in *file*.
	   -o *file* use only the words in *file*.
	   -r use first field of each input line as a reference id appended to each output line. Do not permute.
	   -t prepare the output to be phototypeset.
	   -w *n* change the line length to *n* (default is 72).

pwd	**pwd** Print the full pathname of the current directory. (In the C Shell, the built-in command **dirs** is much faster.)

pxp *options name*.**p**   **pxp**

Format or profile a Pascal program.

options

-**a**   include all procedures and functions.

-**c** *cfile*
          use core file *cfile* for the profile data.

-**d**   include declarations.

-**e**   remove the include statements and replace
          with the contents of the include files.

-**f**   fully parenthesize expressions.

-**j**   left justify procedures and functions.

-**L**   use only lower case for keywords and iden-
          tifiers.

-**n**   use new pages for include files.

-**s**   remove comments.

-**t**   produce procedure and function call
          counts.

-**u**   use only the first 72 characters on each
          line.

-**w**   suppress warning messages.

-**z** *name* . . .
          produce the execution profile for all func-
          tions and procedures, or for the functions
          and procedures with the specified *names*.

-**_**   underline keywords.

-*n*   indent *n* spaces for pretty format.

---

ratfor [*options*] [*files*]   **ratfor**

Convert rational FORTRAN to irrational FORTRAN.

options

-**C**   retain comments in the translated version.

-**h**   convert strings to Hollerith constants.

-**6***c*   change the continuation character to *c*.

---

red [*options*] [*file*]   **red**

Restricted version of **ed**. With **red**, only files in the
current working directory can be edited. Shell commands using **!** are not allowed.

---

refer

refer [*options*]

Preprocessor for **nroff** and **troff** to find and format references.

options

-a[*n*]   reverse all or the first *n* author's names.

-b   omit numbers and labels in text.

-c *string*
    capitalize fields whose key letters are in *string*.

-e   accumulate references and write as:
```
.[
$LIST$
.]
```

-kx   use labels in a reference data line beginning with %*x* (default is L).

-l[*m,n*]
    use author's last name and publication date for references. Only the first *m* letters of the last name and the last *n* digits of the date are used.

-p*file*   search *file* before the default file.

-n   do not search the default file.

-s*file*   sort references by fields whose key letters are in *file*.

regcmp

regcmp [*option*] *files*

Compile the regular expressions in one or more *files* and place the output in *file*.i. The output is C source code. Entries in *files* are of the form:

      C variable   "*regular expression*"

option

-   place the output in *file*.c.

rm

rm [*options*] *files*

Delete one or more *files*. To remove a file, you must have write permission in the directory that contains the file, but you need not have permission on the file itself. If you do not have write permission on the file, you will be prompted (**y** or **n**) to override.

options		<div align="right">**rm** *continued*</div>

    -f   remove files unconditionally.

    -i   prompt for "y" (remove the file) or "n" (do not remove the file).

    -r   if *file* is a directory, remove the entire directory and all its contents, including subdirectories. Be forewarned: use of this option can be very dangerous.

    -   use this option before a list of filenames which includes a filename beginning with "-".

---

rmdel -r*sid files*   **rmdel**

Remove a delta from one or more SCCS *files*, where *sid* is the SCCS id version number.

---

rmdir *directories*   **rmdir**

Delete entries for *directories*. *directories* must be empty. They are deleted from the parent directory. To remove a directory that is not empty, use **rm -r**.

---

rsh   **rsh**

The **rsh** command is a restricted version of **sh** that is intended to be used where security is important. See the **sh** command.

---

sact *files*   **sact**

Report impending deltas to the SCCS *files*. If *files* are directories, **sact** operates on all files in those directories. If *files* is given as **-**, the standard input is read. **sact** will list five output fields. See Section 9 for more information on SCCS.

---

sag [*options*]   **sag**

Graphically display system activity data produced with **sar**.

☞

---

sag
continued
	options
	  -e *time*
	    use data previous to *time* (format *hh*[:*mm*]).
	  -f *file* use *file* as the *sar* data source.
	  -i *sec* limit data to *sec* second intervals.
	  -s *time* use data later than *time* (format *hh*[:*mm*]).
	  -T *term*
	    output is for device type *name*.
	  -x *spec*
	    x-axis specification. See *spec* below.
	  -y *spec*
	    y-axis specification. See *spec* below.
	
	spec has the syntax:
	name[*op name*] ... [*lo hi*]
	name a string header matching one in the *sar* re-
	    port.
	op + - * / separated by blanks.
	lo lower axis limit.
	hi upper axis limit.

sar	**sar** [*report options*] [*process options*]
	
	Report system activity data
	report options
	  -a include file access routine data.
	  -A include all data.
	  -b include buffer activity data.
	  -c include system call data.
	  -d include device block data.
	  -m include message and semaphore data.
	  -q include average queue length data.
	  -u include CPU data.
	  -v include process and file table data.
	  -w include system swapping data.
	  -y include *tty* device data.
	
	process options
	Any combination of the **-s**, **-e**, **-i**, or **-f** options as de-
	scribed under **sag**.
	  t [*n*] sample activity counters at *n* intervals of *t*
	    seconds. Default interval is 1. *t* must be
	    specified if none of the options **-s**, **-e**, **-i**, or
	    -f are specified.

-o *file* send samples, in binary form, to *file*; use only with *t* [*n*]	**sar** *continued*

---

scat *options files* — **scat**

Send files to a synchronous printer.

options

- **-s** silent mode.
- **-u** unbuffered mode.

---

scc — **scc**

Stand-alone compilation for C programs. All options for **cc** are valid.

options

- **-p** create unexecutable output.
- **+[lib]** define the device configuration library.

---

sccsdiff -r*sid1* **-r***sid2* [*options*] [*diffopts*] *files* — **sccsdiff**

Report the differences of two versions of an SCCS *file*. **r***sid1* and **r***sid2* identify the deltas to be compared in the SCCS file(s). See Section 9 for more information on SCCS.

options

- **-p** pipe output through **pr**.
- **-s***n* file segment size is *n*.

diffopts

diff options **-b, -c, -e, -f,** and **-h** can follow the **sccsdiff** options.

---

sdb [*options*] [*objfile* [*corefile* [*dir-list*]]] — **sdb**

A C and FORTRAN symbolic debugging program used to look at "core" files resulting from aborted programs. *objfile* contains an executable program and *corefile* contains the core image produced when *objfile* was executed. **a.out** is the default *objfile*. **core** is the default *corefile*. The *dir-list* argument specifies the source directory for the files compiled to create *objfile*. See Section 8 for more information on **sdb**.

☞

sdb
continued
	options
	    -w open *objfile* for modification.
	    -W suppress warning messages.

sdiff

sdiff [*options*] *file1 file2*

Produce a side-by-side comparison of *file1* with *file2*.
The output is

text text	identical lines.
text <	line exists only in *file1*.
> *text*	line exists only in *file2*.
text | *text*	lines are different.

options

-l   list only lines of *file1* that are identical.

-o *outfile*
> send identical lines of *file1* and *file2* to *out-file*; print line differences and edit *outfile* by entering, when prompted, the following commands:
>
> e   edit an empty file.
> e b edit both left and right columns.
> e l edit left column.
> e r edit right column.
> l   append left column to outfile.
> q   exit the editor.
> r   append right column to outfile.
> s   do not print identical lines ("silent mode").
> v   turn off "silent mode."

-s   do not print identical lines.

-w*n* set line length to *n* (default is usually 130).

sed

sed [*options*] [*files*]

Edit one or more *files* using the commands listed from
files or from standard input. See Section 4 for more
information on **sed**.

options

-e *script*
> execute commands in *script*.

-f_file_	take script from _file_.	**sed**
-n	suppress default output.	_continued_

setup

The first user of a system can login as **setup**, or if already logged in, can issue the **setup** command to add users and passwords to the system.

sh [_options_] [_commands_]

The standard command interpreter which executes _commands_ from a terminal or a file. See Section 2 for more information on the shell.

options

-a	mark export variables.
-c _cmd_	execute command _cmd_.
-e	terminate if a command exits.
-f	disable file generation.
-h	hash functions as they are defined.
-i	interactive shell.
-k	place all arguments in the environment.
-n	read command but do not execute.
-r	restricted shell.
-s	read command from the standard input.
-t	exit after executing one command.
-u	set error when substituting unset variables.
-v	print all shell lines as they are read.
-x	print commands and arguments when executed.

shl

Control more than one shell (layer) from a single terminal. From the **shl** prompt level, the following commands may be issued:

block _name_ [_name2_ ...]
    block the layer _name_.
create [_name_]
    create the layer _name_.
delete _name_ [_name2_ ...]
    delete the layer _name_.

shl
continued

help or **?**
> provide **shl** command syntax.

layers [**-l**] [*name* . . .]
> · print information about layers. The **-l** option provides a **ps**-like display.

name use *name* as the current level.

quit exit **shl** and kill all the layers.

resume [*name*]
> return to the last layer or the layer *name*.

toggle flip back to the previous layer.

unblock *name* [*name2* . . .]
> do not block the layer *name*.

---

shutdown

shutdown [*options*] [*time*]

Terminate all processes and take system down to single-user mode after *time* seconds (default is usually 60 seconds).

options

-**h** execute halt.
-**k** issue *shutdown* messages, but do not shutdown the system.
-**r** execute reboot.

Syntax of this command is system-specific.

---

size

size [*options*] [*objfile* . . .]

Print the (decimal) number of bytes of each *objfile*. If *objfile* is not specified, **a.out** is used.

options

-**o** octal output.
-**x** hexadecimal output.
-**V** report the *size* program version number.

---

sleep

sleep *seconds*

Wait for a specified number of *seconds*.

sort [*options*] [*files*] **sort**

Sort the lines of the named *files* in alphabetical order.

options

-b	ignore leading spaces and tabs.
-c	verify the input file.
-d	sort in dictionary order.
-f	fold upper to lower case.
-i	ignore characters outside the ASCII 040-176 range.
-m	merge sorted input files.
-M	compare first three characters as months.
-n	sort in arithmetic order.
-o *file*	put output in *file*.
-r	reverse the order of the sort.
-t*c*	separate fields with *c* (default is tab).
-u	identical lines in input file appear only one (unique) time in output.

-y*kmem*

adjust the amount of memory *sort* uses. If *kmem* is not specified the maximum memory is allocated.

-z*recsz*

provide the maximum number of bytes for any one line in the file. This options prevents abnormal termination of *sort* in certain cases.

+*pos1* [**-***pos2*]

sort only from *pos1* to *pos2*. If *pos2* is missing, sort to end of line.

---

spell [*options*] [*files*] **spell**

Compare the words of one or more named *files* with the system dictionary and report all misspelled words.

options

-b	check for British spelling.
-i	ignore files included with the **nroff** or **troff** .so request.
-l	follow include files (this is the default).
-v	print words not in the dictionary.
-x	print every possible stem for each word.

spell *continued*	+*file* do not output the words in the sorted *file*.

spline	**spline** [*options*]
	
	Create a "smooth" function from the input abscissas and ordinates. The output is also a set of abscissas and ordinates.
	    -a add abscissas automatically.
	    -k*n* use *n* for the constant value in the boundary computation.
	    -*n* use *n* intervals between the upper and lower x limits.
	    -p create periodic output.
	    -x*low* [*up*]
	          lower and upper *x* limits.

split	**split** [*option*] [*ifile*] [*ofile*] Split *ifile* into a specified number of line segments and write the results to *ofile***aa**, *ofile***bb**, *etc. (Default is* **xaa, xab,** *etc.)* *option* -*n* split *ifile* into *n* line segments (default is 1000).
starter	**starter** Provide five categories of UNIX information for new users.

strip	**strip** [*options*] *files*
	
	Remove the symbol table and relocation bits from object files *files*.
	options
	    -b leave static symbol, external symbol, and scoping information.
	    -l strip only line number information.
	    -r leave static symbol, external symbol, and relocation information.

-V	report the *strip* program version number.	**strip**
-x	leave static and external symbol information.	*continued*

---

stty [*options*] [*modes*]

stty

Set terminal I/O options for the current device. Without options, **stty** reports the terminal settings. As superuser, you can set or read settings from another device using the syntax:

> **stty** ⌊*options*⌋ [*modes*] < *device*

options

> **-a**   report all option settings.
> **-g**   report current settings.

control modes

> **0**   hang up phone
> *n*   set terminal baud rate to *n*.
> **[-]clocal**
> > [enable]disable modem control.
>
> **[-]cread**
> > [disable]enable the receiver.
>
> **cs***n*   select character size.
> **[-]cstopb**
> > [one]two stop bits per character.
>
> **[-]hup** [do not]hang up connection on last close.
> **[-]hupcl**
> > [do not]hang up connection on last close.
>
> **[-]loblk**
> > [do not]block layer output.
>
> **[-]parenb**
> > [disable]enable parity generation and detection.
>
> **[-]parodd**
> > use [even]odd parity.

input modes

> **[-]brkint**
> > [do not]signal INTR on break.
>
> **[-]icrnl**
> > map CR to NL on input.
>
> **[-]ignbrk**
> > [do not]ignore break on input.

[-]igncr
> [do not]ignore CR on input.

[-]ignpar
> [do not]ignore parity errors.

[-]inlcr
> [do not]map NL to CR on input.

[-]inpck
> [disable]enable input parity checking.

[-]istrip
> [do not]strip input characters to seven bits.

[-]iuclc
> [do not]map uppercase to lowercase on input.

[-]ixany
> allow [XON]any character to restart output.

[-]ixoff
> [do not]send START/STOP characters when queue is nearly empty/full.

[-]ixon
> [disable]enable START/STOP output control.

[-]parmrk
> [do not]mark parity errors.

output modes

bs$n$
> select style of delay for backspaces (0 or 1).

cr$n$
> select style of delay for carriage returns (0-3).

ff
> select style of delay for form feeds (0 or 1).

nl
> select style of delay for line feeds (0-1).

[-]ocrnl
> [do not]map NL to CR-NL on output.

[-]ofdel
> set fill character to [NULL]DEL.

[-]ofill
> delay output with [timing]fill characters.

[-]olcuc
> [do not]map lowercase to uppercase on output.

[-]onlcr
> [do not]map NL to CR-NL on output.

[-]onlret
> [do not]perform CR after NL.

[-]onocr

do[not] output CRs at column zero.

[-]opost

[do not]post-process output; ignore all other output modes.

tab*n* select style of delay for horizontal tabs (0-3).

vt*n* select style of delay for vertical tabs (0 or 1).

local modes

[-]echo

[do not]echo every character typed.

[-]echoe

[do not]echo ERASE character as BS-space-BS string.

[-]echok

[do not]echo NL after KILL character.

[-]echonl

[do not]echo NL.

[-]icanon

[disable]enable canonical input (ERASE and KILL processing).

[-]isig [disable]enable checking of characters against INTR and QUIT.

[-]noflsh

[enable]disable flush after INTR or QUIT.

[-]stappl

[line]application mode on a synchronous line.

[-]stflush

[disable]enable flush on synchronous line.

[-]stwrap

[enable]disable truncation on synchronous line.

[-]xcase

[do not]change case on local output.

control assignments

ctrlchar c

set control character to *c*. *ctrlchar* is: **ctab, eof, eol, erase, intr, kill, quit, min, time**

line *iP* set line discipline to *i* (0-127).

☞

stty
continued

combination modes

cooked
same as **-raw**.

[-]evenp
same as **[-]parenb** and **cs[8]7**.

ek   reset ERASE and KILL characters to # and @.

[-]lcase
[un]set **xcase, iuclc,** and **olcuc**.

[-]LCASE
same as **[-]lcase**.

[-]nl [un]set **icrnl** and **onlcr**. **-nl** also unsets **inlcr, igncr, ocrnl,** and **onlretP**.

[-]oddp
same as **[-]parenb, cs7[8],** and **[no]parodd**.

[-]parity
same as **[-]parenb** and **cs[8]7**

[-]raw [disable]enable raw input and output (no ERASE, KILL, INTR, QUIT, EOT, or output post processing).

sane   reset all modes to reasonable values.

[-]tabs
[expand to spaces]preserve output tabs.

term   set all modes suitable for terminal type *term* (tty33, tty37, vt05, tn300, ti700, or tek).

---

su

su [-] [*user*] [*-c command*]

Create a shell with the effective user id of another *user*. If no *user* is specified, create a superuser shell. Enter ^D to terminate.

options

-   go through the entire login sequence. Note that, if present, this option must occur before the specified user name.

-c *command*
execute *command* via the shell. If *command* is followed by options or arguments, the entire string should be quoted.

sum [*option*] *files*   **sum**

Calculate and print a checksum and the number of blocks for the named *files*.

option

   -r   use alternate checksum algorithm.

---

sync   **sync**

Update the super block. **sync** should be called to insure file system integrity before the system is shut down.

---

sysadm [*options*]   **sysadm**

Enter the system administration command menus. System administration tasks are performed by selecting menu items.

---

tabs [*tabspec*] [**+m**n] [**-T** *type*]   **tabs**

Set terminal tab stops according to *tabspec*.

tabspec

-*n*	repetitive spec at columns (e.g., 1+n, 1+2*n, etc.).
n1,n2,...	arbitrary ascending values. If *n* is preceded by +, it is added.
-a	1,10,16,36,72.
-a2	1,10,16,40,72.
-c	1,8,12,16,20,55.
-c2	1,6,10,14,49.
-c3	1,6,10,14,18,22,26,30,34, 38,42,46,50,54,58,62,67.
-f	1,7,11,15,19,23.
-p	1,5,9,13,17,21,25,29,33, 37,41,45,49,53,57,61.
-s	1,10,55.
-u	1,12,20,44.
-*file*	read first line of *file* for tabs.
+mn	set left margin to *n* (default is 10).

tabs *continued*	**-T** *type* terminal *type*.

tail

tail [*options*] [*file*]

Print the last ten lines of the named *file*.

options

-f   do not terminate at the end of file.

+*n*[**lbc**]

    begin at *n*th line (default), block, or character from beginning of file. Print to end of file.

-*n*[**lbc**]

    begin at *n*th line (default), block, or character from end of file. Print to end of file.

tar

tar [*options*] [*files*]

Copy and restore multiple *files* to or from tape.

function options (choose one)

c   create a new tape.

r   append *files* to tape.

t   print the names of *files* if they are stored on the tape (if *files* not specified, print names of all files).

u   add files if not on tape or if modified.

x   extract *files* from tape (if *files* not specified, extract all files).

options

b*n*   use *n* for blocking factor (maximum is 20, default is 1).

f*file*   use *file* as archive (default is **/dev/mt?**).

l   print link resolution error messages.

m   do not restore modification times.

n   select tape drive *n* (0-7, default is 1).

v   print function letter (*x* for extraction or *a* for archive) and name of files.

w   wait for confirmation (y).

tbl [*option*] [*files*]   **tbl**

A preprocessor for *nroff* and *troff* that formats tables
contained in *files* and enclosed by **.TS** and **.TE** requests. See Section 7 for more information on **tbl**.

options

   -TX   use only full vertical line motions.

---

tc *options file*   **tc**

Simulate phototypesetter output on a Tektronix 4014
terminal.

options

   -pn   use page length *n*.
   -sn   skip the first *n* pages.
   -t   do not wait for new-lines at end of page.

---

tee [*options*] [*files*]   **tee**

Duplicate the standard input and send one copy to the
standard output and one copy to *files*.

options

   -a   append output to *files*.
   -i   ignore all interrupts.

---

test *expression*   **test**
or [*expression*]

Evaluate an *expression* and, if its value is true, return a
zero exit status; otherwise, a non-zero exit status is returned. In shell scripts, you can use the alternate form
[*expression*]. This command is generally used with
conditional constructs in shell programs. See Section
2 for more information on **test**.

---

time *command* [*arguments*]   **time**

Execute a *command* with optional arguments and print
the total elapsed time, execution time, process execution time, and system time of the process.

---

timex

timex [*options*] *command* [*arguments*]

Execute a *command* with optional arguments and print information specified by the **time** command. Report process data with various options.

options

-**p**   report process accounting information with possible *suboptions*.

-**o**   report total number of blocks and characters used.

-**s**   report total system activity.

suboptions for -**p**

-**f**   include fork/exit flag and system exit status.

-**h**   report the fraction of CPU time instead of mean memory size.

-**k**   report the total core-minutes instead of the mean memory size.

-**m**   report mean core size.

-**r**   report CPU use computation.

-**t**   report user and system CPU times.

touch

touch [*options*] [*date*] *files*

Update the access and modification time and date to the current time, or the optional *date*, for one or more *files*.

options

-**a**   update only the access time.

-**c**   do not create non-existent files.

-**m**   update only the modification time.

date

the date and time, in the format: mmddhhmm[yy].

tplot

tplot [-T*terminal* [-**e** *raster*]]

Read plotting instructions from the standard input and produce instructions suitable for *terminal*. With no *terminal* specified, the environment parameter **$TERM** is used by default.

The **-e** option sends a scan-converted file *raster* to the plotter. It is used only when *terminal* is **ver**, specifying the Versatec D1200A.

tplot
continued

---

tput [*option*] *capname*

tput

Print the value of the terminal capability *capname* from the *terminfo* source.

option

    -T*type*
            information for terminal *type* (default is the terminal in use).

    capname
            a terminfo capability such as **clear** or **col**.

---

tr [*options*] [*string1* [*string2*]]

tr

Substitute characters found in *string1* into *string2*.

options

    -c   complement characters in *string1* with ASCII 001-377.
    -d   delete characters in *string1* from output.
    -s   squeeze repeated output characters in *string2*.

---

troff [*options*] [*files*]

troff

Format *files* for printing on a phototypesetter.

options

    -a   use printable ASCII approximation.
    -b   report phototypesetter status.
    -f   do not feed out paper at end of run.
    -i   read standard input after files.
    -m*name*
            prepend **/usr/lib/tmac/tmac.***name* to files.
    -n*n*   number first page *n*.
    -o*list* print only pages contained in the comma-separated *list*. A page range is specified by *n-m*.
    -p*n*   print all characters in point size *n*.

☞

---

troff *continued*	**-q** do not echo **.rd** requests. **-r** *an* assign *n* to register *a*. **-s***n* stop every *n* pages. **-t** send output to standard output. **-w** if the phototypesetter is busy, wait until it is free.
true	**true** Return a successful exit status. See also **false**.
tsort	**tsort** [*file*] Perform a topological sort on a *file*.

tty	**tty** [*option*]
	
	Print the device name of your terminal.
	options
	     -l print the synchronous line number.
	     -s return only the codes:
	            0 = a terminal.
	            1 = not a terminal.
	            2 = invalid options used.

umask	**umask** [*value*] Print the current value or set the file creation mode mask to *value*. *value* is a three-digit octal code specifying the read-write-execute permissions to be turned off. This is the opposite of **chmod**. For example, **umask** 002 produces -rw-rw-r--, and **umask** 077 produces -rw-------. Usually used in *.login* or *.profile*. See Section 2 for more information.
umount	**umount** *options* See the **mount** command.

uname [*options*]   **uname**

Print the current UNIX system name.

options

    -a   report all of the following information:

    -m   the hardware name.

    -n   the node name.

    -r   the operating system release.

    -s   the system name.

    -S*name*

           change the nodename to *name*. Use with-
           out any other options. (This option does
           not work on all systems.)

    -v   print the operating system version.

---

unget [*options*] *files*   **unget**

Restore a previous **get** for one or more SCCS *files*. See
Section 9 for more information on SCCS.

options

    -n   do not remove file retrieved with **get**.

    -r *sid* the SCCS id version number.

    -s   suppress standard output.

---

uniq [*options*[*arguments*]] [*file1* [*file2*]]   **uniq**

Remove duplicate adjacent lines from *file1* and write
the remainder to *file2*. Often used as a filter.

options

    -c   print unique lines and count repeated lines.

    -d   print only one copy of repeated lines.

    -u   print only unique lines in *file1*.

arguments

    -*n*   ignore first *n* fields of a line.

    +*n*   ignore first *n* characters of a field. **-n** and
           +n are not used alone, but with the first
           three options.

units	**units** Interactively supply a formula to convert a number from one unit to another. The file **/usr/lib/units** gives a complete list of the units. Use ˆ**D** to exit.
unpack	**unpack** *files* Expand one or more *files*, created with **pack**, to their original form. See **pcat** and **pack**.

usage	**usage** [*options*] [*command*]
	
	Interactively retrieve information about *command*. If the user does not supply a *command*, a menu is supplied from which the user can list the available commands.
	
	options
	
	  -d provide a description of *command*.
	  -e provide examples of the use of *command*.
	  -o provide the options for *command*.

uucp	**uucp** [*options*] [*source*!]*file* [*destination*!]*file*
	
	Copy a file (or group of files) from the source to the destination. The "source" and "destination" can be remote systems. The destination file can be a directory.
	
	options
	
	  -c do not copy files to the spool directory.
	  -C copy files to the spool directory.
	  -d make directories for the copy when they do not exist (default).
	  -f do not make directories when they do not exist.
	  -g*x* set priority of transfer. If *x* is a "low" character such as "a" or "b", the job will be transferred before other jobs waiting to be sent. This also applies to numerical *x* where *x* is a "low" number.
	  -j print the **uucp** job number.
	  -m send mail when the copy is complete.

-n*user*
>   send mail to *user* when the copy is complete.

-r   queue the job but do not start communication program (**uucico**).

-s*file*   send transfer status to *file* (a full pathname).

-x*n*   specify the level of debugging output desired to be *n*, $0 \le n \le 9$. High numbers give more output.

uucp
continued

---

uulog [*options*]

Print information from the *uucp* log file.

options

-f*system*
>   print the most recent commands for *system*.

-s*system*
>   print all commands for *system*.

uulog

---

uuname [*option*]

Print the names of the systems *uucp* knows about.

option

-l   print the local system's node name.

uuname

---

uupick [*option*] *system*

Query the status of files sent to the user with **uuto**.

option

-s*system*
>   search only for files sent from *system*.

interactive response

<new-line>
>   move to next entry.

a[*dir*] move all files sent from *system* to the named *directory*.

m[*dir*]
>   move the file to the directory *dir*.

uupick

☞

---

uupick *continued*	**p** print the file. **q** quit **uupick**. **EOT(control-D)** quit **uupick**. **!***cmd* execute the shell command *cmd*.

uustat

uustat [*options*]

Provide information about **uucp** requests. This command can also be used to cancel **uucp** requests. The **-a, -k, -m, -p, -q,** and **-r** options can only be used individually.

options

- **-a**   report all queued jobs.
- **-k***jobn*
  - kill request *jobn*.
- **-m**   report accessibility of other systems.
- **-p**   execute a "ps -flp" on the active communications processes.
- **-q**   report the number of jobs queued for all systems.
- **-r***jobn* touch the files associated with *jobn*.
- **-s***system*
  - report the status of jobs for *system*.
- **-u***user*
  - report the status of jobs for *user*.

uuto

uuto [*options*] *sourcefiles destination*

Send source files to a destination, where *destination* is of the form *system!user*. The user on the destination system can pick up the files with **uupick**.

options

- **-m**   send mail when the copy is complete.
- **-p**   copy files to the spool directory.

uux

uux [*options*] [[*sys*]**!** *command*]

Gather files from various systems and execute *command* on the specified machine, *sys*.

options

-     use standard input.

-a*user*
    notify *user* upon completion.

-b   print the standard input when the exit status indicates an error.

-c   do not copy files to the spool directory.

-C   copy files to the spool directory.

-g*c*/*n* set priority of transfer. If *c* is a "low" character such as "a" or "b", the job will be transferred before other jobs waiting to be sent. This also applies to *n* where *n* is a "low" number.

-j   print the **uucp** job number.

-n   inhibit *mail* notification.

-p   use standard input.

-r   queue the job but do not start communication program (**uucico**).

-s*file* send transfer status to *file* (a full pathname).

-x*num*
    specify the level of debugging output desired to be *n*, $0 \le n \le 9$. Higher numbers give more output.

-z   notify the user when complete.

---

val [*options*] *file* . . .

val

Validate that the SCCS *file* meets the characteristics specified in the options. **val** produces messages on the standard output for each *file* and returns an 8-bit code upon exit. See Section 9 for more information on SCCS.

options

-     a special option used alone on the command line. Read standard input and interpret each line as a **val** command line. Exit with an end-of-file condition.

-m*name*
    compare *name* with %M% keyword in *file*.

-r*sid* check whether the SCCS delta number, *sid*, is ambiguous or invalid.

val *continued*	**-s** silence any error message. **-y***type* compare *type* with %Y% keyword in *file*.

vc

vc [*options*] [*keyword=value* ...]

Copy lines from standard input to standard output under control of the **vc** keywords and arguments within the standard input.

options

    -a   replace control keywords in all lines, including text lines.

    -c*char*
        use *char* as the control character.

    -s   suppress warning messages.

    -t   if any control characters are found before the first tab in the file, remove all characters up to the first tab.

vedit

vedit [*options*] [*files*]

Same as **vi**, but with the **showmode** and **novice** flags set, and the **report** flag set to 1. Intended for beginners.

vi

vi [*options*] [*files*]

A screen-oriented text editor based on **ex**. See Section 4 for more information on **vi** and **ex**.

options

    -r*file* retrieve last saved version of named *file* after crash.

    -R   read-only mode.

    -t *tag* begin editing named *file* at location *tag*.

    -w*n*   set default window size to *n*.

    -x   edit an encrypted file.

    +[*n*][*pattern*]
        position cursor at end of file, line number *n*, or *pattern*.

    +*command*
        interpret the specified **ex** *command* before editing.

view [*options*] [*files*]   **view**

Same as **vi -R**.

---

wait [*n*]   **wait**

Wait for all background processes to complete and report their termination status. If *n* is specified, wait
only for the process with process id *n*. Used in shell
scripts.

---

wall   **wall**
message

Send a message to all users. End message with ˆD.

---

wc [*options*] [*files*]   **wc**

Print a character, word, and line count for *files*. If *file*
is not given, the standard input is used.

options

    -c   character count only.
    -l   line count only.
    -w   word count only.

---

what [*options*] *files*   **what**

Search the given files for occurrences of the pattern
get substitutes for **%Z%**, and print out the following
text. See Section 9 for more information on SCCS.

options

    -s   quit after finding the first occurrence of a
           pattern.

---

who [*options*] [*file*]   **who**

Display information about the current status of the system. With no options, list the names of users currently
logged onto the system.

    -a   use all options.

who *continued*	**-b**	report information about the last reboot.
	-d	report expired processes.
	-H	print headings.
	-l	report inactive terminal lines.
	-p	report previously spawned processes.
	-q	limit display to user names.
	-r	report the run level.
	-s	list the name, line and time fields.
	-t	report the last system clock change.
	-T	report the logged in terminals.
	-u	report the logged in terminals and the *state* of the lines.
	am i	print the user name you are logged in as.

---

write

write *user* [*tty*]
message

Initiate or respond to an interactive conversation with *user*. A write session is terminated with ^D.

tty   the *tty* number if the user is logged on to more than one terminal.

---

xargs

xargs [*options*] [*command* [*initial_args*]]

Combine the fixed *initial_args* with arguments read from standard input to execute the specified *command*. Used to pass a command more arguments than it can normally handle. For example,

find / -user *user* **-print | xargs grep** *pattern*

will invoke grep to search for *pattern* on all files on the system belonging to *user*.

options

-e *eof*   set *eof*, the end-of-file string (default is underscore).

-i *replace*
   execute command with occurrences of *replace*. Standard input replaced by initial arguments.

-l *n*   execute command for *n* lines of arguments.

-n *n*   execute command with up to *n* arguments.

-p   prompt for execution of each command (**y** confirms execution).

-s*size* maximum *size* of argument list.	**xargs**
-t trace mode.	*continued*
-x terminate if argument list greater than size.	

yacc [*options*] *file*   **yacc**

Yet another compiler-compiler.

options

-d   generate **y.tab.h** with **#define** statements.

-l   do not include any **#line** constructs in the code produced.

-t   compile runtime debugging code by default.

-v   produce **y.output**.

2

Shell Syntax

- **The Bourne Shell**
- **The C Shell**

    The following subsections are provided for each shell:

    - Special Files
    - Filename Metacharacters
    - Variable Substitution
    - Special Symbols
    - Shell Variables
    - Built-in Commands

- **Comparison of Bourne and C Shells**

The Bourne Shell

Special Files

$HOME/.profile	executed automatically at login

Filename Metacharacters

*	match any string of zero or more characters
?	match any single character
[*abc* . . .]	match any one of the enclosed characters. A pair of characters separated by a dash will match any character lexically between the pair.
![*abc* . . .]	match any character *not* enclosed as above

Variable Substitution

variable=value . . .	set *variable* to *value*
$*variable*	use value of *variable*
$*variable*[:]-*value*	use *variable* if set; otherwise set to *value*
$*variable*[:]=*value*	use *variable* if set; otherwise set to *value* and assign *value* to *variable*
$*variable*[:]?*value*	use *variable* if set; otherwise print *value*, then exit
$*variable*[:]+*value*	use *value* if *variable* is set; otherwise nothing

If the colon (:) is included in the above expressions then a test is performed to see if the variable is non-null as well as set. Note that there should be no spaces used in the above expressions.

Shell Variables

The following variables are automatically set by the shell. (Note that the $ is not actually part of the variable name. Any of the substitution patterns shown above can be used.)

$#	number of command line arguments
$-	options supplied in invocation or by the set command
$?	exit value of last executed command
$$	exit process number of current process
$!	exit process number of last background command
$1 . . . $9	arguments on command line
$*	all arguments on command line ("$1 $2 . . . ")
$@	all arguments on command line, individually quoted ("$1" "$2" . . .)

The following variables are used by the shell but are not automatically set.

CDPATH	directories searched by **cd**
HOME	home directory defined in **passwd** file
IFS	internal field separators; default space, tab and newline
MAIL	default mail file
MAILCHECK	number of seconds between periodic mail checks
MAILPATH	files checked for mail, delimited by colon
PATH	search path for commands (default is **:/bin:/usr/bin**)
PS1	primary prompt string; default is $
PS2	secondary prompt string; default is >
SHACCT	file to write accounting information
SHELL	name of the shell
TERM	terminal type

⎯Special Symbols⎯⎯⎯⎯⎯⎯⎯⎯⎯⎯⎯⎯⎯⎯⎯⎯⎯⎯⎯

I	perform pipeline (use output of preceding command as input of following command, e.g., **cat** *file* I **lpr**)
;	separate sequential commands on same line
&	run command in background (e.g., **lpr** *file*&)
&&	execute command if previous command was successful (e.g., **grep** *string file* && **lpr** *file*)
II	execute command if previous command was unsuccessful (e.g., **grep** *string1 file* II **grep** *string2 file*)
( )	execute commands enclosed in ( ) in a subshell; output from the entire set can then be redirected as a unit or placed in the background. Commands should be separated by ; within the parens.
{ }	execute commands enclosed in { } in current shell
name ( ) {*cmds*}	define function *name*
´...´	take all characters between single quotation marks literally; don't allow special character meaning.
\	take following character literally
"..."	take enclosed characters literally but allow variable and command substitution
`cmd`	use output of *cmd* as argument to another command
#	begin a comment in a shell file
<*file*	take input from *file*
<<*string*	read standard input up to a line identical to *string*
>*file*	redirect output to *file* (overwrite)
>>*file*	redirect output to end of *file* (append)
<&*n*	duplicate standard input from *n* e.g. 2<&3
<&–	close standard input
n>	redirect output from *n* instead of default 1
n<	redirect input from *n* instead of default 0

Built-In Bourne Shell Commands

:	**:** Null command. Returns an exit status of 0.
.	**.** *file* Read and execute indicated *file*. *file* does not have to be executable.
break	**break** [*n*] Exit from a **for** or **while** for the *n* innermost levels.

case	**case** *value* **in**
	    pattern [|*pattern*]) *cmd*;;
	        ⋮
	  pattern [|*pattern*]) *cmd*;;
	esac
	
	Execute each *cmd* for which *value* matches the specified *pattern*. If a second pattern is specified (preceded by a |), execute *cmd* if *value* matches either pattern. Patterns can use file generation meta-characters.

cd	**cd** [*dir*] Change working directory to *dir*; default is home directory of user.
continue	**continue** [*n*] Resume *n*-th enclosing **for** or **while** loop.

echo *string*

Write *string* to standard output. The following **echo** escape characters have special meaning in the Bourne shell:

\b	backspace
\c	suppress terminating newline
\f	formfeed
\n	newline
\r	carriage return
\t	tab character
****	backslash
nnn	character with ASCII value *nnn*, *nnn* an octal number of 1 to 3 digits beginning with 0.

These escapes must be quoted so they are not interpreted directly by the shell.

eval [*args*]

Evaluate *args* as a command line and use the result as input to the shell.

exec [*command*]

Execute *command* in place of current shell.

exit [*n*]

Exit the shell with exit status *n*, e.g. **exit 1**. If *n* is not given, exit status will be that of last command given.

export [*variable* ...]

Export *variable* to environment of subsequently executed commands. If no argument is given, the list of exportable variables is printed.

for	**for** *variable* [**in** *list*] **do** *commands* **done** For variable *x* (in optional *list* of values) do *commands*. If *list* is omitted, $@ is assumed.
hash	**hash** [**-r**] [*commands*] Search for *commands* and note where they are located, or if *commands* are not specified, list current hashed commands. The **-r** option will remove *commands* from the hash list.

if	**if** *condition1*
	then *commands1*
	[**elif** *condition2*
	    then *commands2*]
	    ⋮
	[**else** *commands3*]
	fi
	
	If *condition1* is met, do *commands1*; else if *condition2* is met, do *commands2*; if neither is met, do *commands3*. Conditions are usually specified with the **test** command.

login	**login** [*user*] Log in as another user.
newgrp	**newgrp** [*group*] Change the group id of the caller.

     Built-In Bourne Shell Commands

pwd

Print the present working directory to standard output.

---

read *variable1* [*variable2* ...]

Read one line of standard input, and assign each word to the corresponding *variable*, with all leftover words assigned to last variable. If only one variable is specified, the entire line will be assigned to that variable.

---

readonly [*variable1* *variable2* ...]

Specify *variables* as read only, or list current read only variables.

---

return [*n*]

Stop execution of function with exit status *n*, or with exit status of previously executed command.

---

set [*options*[[--] *arg* ...]]

With no arguments **set** prints the values of all variables known to the current shell. The following options can be enabled (–option) or disabled (+option). Specifying -- before listing arguments will prevent those beginning with – from being interpreted as options.

a	Automatically export all subsequently defined variables
e	Exit in bad status if non-interactive
f	Disable file name generation
h	Remember location of commands used in functions as they are defined

☞

---

set *continued*	**k**	Put keywords in an environment for a command
	n	Read but do not execute commands
	t	Exit after one command is executed
	u	Treat unset variables as an error
	v	Print input lines as they are read
	x	Print commands when executed
	arg ...	
		Assigned in order to **$1, $2,** ...

---

shift

shift [*n*]

Shift positional arguments; e.g. **$2** becomes **$1**. If *n* is specified, shift to the left *n* places.

---

test

test *expression* [| *expression*]
or [*expression*]

Evaluate an *expression* and, if its value is true, return a zero exit status; otherwise, return a non-zero exit status. An alternate form of the command uses "[ ]" rather than the word *test*.
The following primitives are used to construct *expression*.

- **-b** *file* true if *file* exists and is a block special file
- **-c** *file* true if *file* exists and is a character special file
- **-d** *file* true if *file* exists and is a directory
- **-f** *file* true if *file* exists and is a regular file
- **-g** *file* true if *file* exists and its set-group-id bit is set
- **-k** *file* true if *file* exists and its sticky bit is set
- **-n** *string*
  true if the length of *string* is non-zero
- **-p** *file* true if *file* exists and is a named pipe (fifo)
- **-r** *file* true if *file* exists and is readable
- **-s** *file* true if *file* exists and has a size greater than zero
- **-t** [*n*] true if the open file whose file descriptor number is *n* (default is 1) is associated with a terminal device

-u *file* true if *file* exists and its set-user-id bit is set

-w *file*

true if *file* exists and is writable

-x *file* true if *file* exists and is executable

-z *s1* true if the length of string *s1* is zero

s1 = *s2*

true if strings *s1* and *s2* are identical

s1 != *s2*

true if strings *s1* and *s2* are *not* identical

string true if *string* is not the null string

n1 op n2

true if comparison *op* between the integers *n1* and *n2* is true. Any of the comparisons **-eq**, **-ne**, **-gt**, **-ge**, **-lt**, and **-le** may be used as *op*.

These primitives may be combined with the negation operator (!), binary *and* (**-a**), binary *or* (**-o**), and parentheses. Operators and operands must be delimited by spaces.

---

times

Print accumulated process times.

---

trap [[*commands*] *signals*]

Execute *commands* if any of *signals* is received. Multiple commands should be quoted as a group and separated by semicolons internally. If *commands* is the null string (i.e., **trap ""** *signals*), then *signals* will be ignored by the shell. If *commands* are omitted entirely, reset processing of specified signals to the default action. If both *commands* and *signals* are omitted, list current trap assignments. Signals are as follows:

0	exit from shell
1	hangup
2	interrupt
3	quit
4	illegal instruction

trap *continued*	**5**	trace trap
	6	IOT instruction
	7	EMT instruction
	8	floating point exception
	10	bus error
	12	bad argument to a system call
	13	write to a pipe without a process to read it
	14	alarm timeout
	15	software termination

type

type *commands*

Print information about specified *commands*.

ulimit

ulimit [*option*] [*n*]

Set the maximum size of files or pipes written by child processes to *n* blocks. Options are **f** (file size, the default) and **p** (pipe size). With no arguments, print the current setting, with **0** signifying no limit.

umask

umask [*nnn*]

Display file creation mask or set file creation mask to octal value *nnn*. The file creation mask determines which permission bits are turned off; e.g., **umask 002** produces **rw-rw-r--**.

unset

unset *names*

Erase definitions of functions or variables listed in *names*.

until

until *condition*
do
        commands
done

Built-In Bourne Shell Commands

Until *condition* is met, do *commands*. *condition* is usually specified with the **test** command.	**until** *continued*

wait [*n*] Wait for process with identification number *n* to terminate and report its status, or for all child processes to finish.	**wait**

while *condition* **do** *commands* **done** While *condition* is met, do *commands*. *Condition* is usually specified with the **test** command.	**while**

filename Read and execute commands from executable file *filename*.	*filename*

The C Shell

Note: The C-shell is not officially part of UNIX System V; however, it is included in one form or another on many systems.

Special Files

~/.cshrc	executed at each instance of shell
~/.login	executed by login shell after .cshrc at login
~/.logout	executed by login shell at logout
/etc/passwd	source of home directories for ~name abbreviations

Filename Metacharacters

*	match any string of zero or more characters
?	match any single character
[...]	match any of the enclosed characters. A pair of characters separated by a dash will match any character lexically between the pair.
{abc, xxx, ... }	match each comma-separated string enclosed in braces; e.g., ls {ch, sec}? might yield ch1 ch2 sec1 sec2.
~	home directory for the current user
~name	substitute home directory of user name

Variable Substitution

In the following substitutions, braces ({ }) can be used to separate a variable name from following characters that would otherwise be a part of it.

$variable ${variable}	use value of variable
$name [n] ${name [n]}	select word number n from name
$#name ${#name}	return the number of words in name
$1 ... $9 ${1} ... ${9}	arguments on command line
$*	all arguments on command line: "$1 ... $9"

The variable substitutions above may be followed by *one* **modifier** from the set:

:g, :h, :r, :t, :x, :gh, :gr, :gt

Modifiers are described more fully later in this section.

$?name ${?name}	return 1 if *name* is set; 0 if *name* is not set
$$	process number of parent shell
$<	read a line from standard input

──Special Symbols─────────────────────────

|	perform pipeline (use output of preceding command as input of following command, e.g., **cat** *file* | **lpr**)
;	separate sequential commands on same line
&	run command in background (e.g., **lpr** *file&*)
&&	execute command if previous command was successful (e.g., **grep** *string file* **&&** **lpr** *file*)
||	execute command if previous command was unsuccessful (e.g., **grep** *string1 file* || **grep** *string2 file*)
'...'	take all characters between single quotation marks literally. (Don't allow special character meaning.)
\	take following character literally
"..."	take enclosed characters literally but allow variable and command substitution
`cmd`	use output of *cmd* as an argument to another command
>!*file*	*redirect to file even when* **noclobber** is set
|&	pipe standard error along with standard output
#	begin a comment in a shell file
<*file*	take input from *file*
<<*string*	read standard input up to a line identical to *string*
>*file*	redirect output to *file*
>>*file*	redirect output to end of *file*
>&*file*	redirect both standard output and standard error to *file*

argv	contains shell argument list of current command
cdpath	can be set to list of directories searched to find a subdirectory if the subdirectory is not in current directory; e.g. "set **cdpath** = (/usr/lib); **cd macros**" is equivalent to "**cd** /usr/lib/macros"
cwd	contains full pathname of current directory
echo	if set, specify each command and argument before execution
histchars	characters to be used by history mechanism
history	can be set to the numeric value for size of history list, e.g. "**set history = 25**"
home	contains the home directory of user
ignoreeof	if set, ignore end-of-file from terminals. This prevents the shell from accidentally being logged out
mail	can be set to specify the file where the shell checks for mail, e.g. "set **mail** = /usr/spool/mail/tim"
noclobber	if set, restrict output redirection to prevent accidental destruction of files
noglob	if set, inhibit filename expansion
nonomatch	if set, it is not an error for filename expansion not to match any existing files
notify	if set, notify size of process completions as they occur; otherwise, notify only when the current job is completed
path	can be set to specify the search path for commands, e.g. "set **path** = (. /usr/bin)"
prompt	the string that is printed before each command is read from interactive input (default is %.) Can be set to reflect current event number from the history list, e.g. "**set prompt = 'tom \!%'.**"
shell	contains the pathname of the shell currently being used
status	contains return status of last command. a value of 0 = normal exit, a value of 1 = command failed.
time	can be set to control automatic timing of commands. If command takes more than $time cpu seconds to execute, then the utilization time is printed for the command; e.g. "**set time = 3.**"
verbose	if set, the words of each command will be printed after history substitution.

Expression Operators

Operators are listed in descending order of precedence.

-, +	unary minus and plus
~	binary inversion
!	logical negation
*, /, %	multiplication, division, modulus
+, -	addition, subtraction
<<, >>	left shift, right shift
<=	less than or equal to
>=	greater than or equal to
<	less than
>	greater than
==	equality (left to right)
!=	inequality
=~	equality in which right hand side is a pattern containing *, ? or [...]
!~	inequality in which right hand side is a pattern containing *, ? or [...]
&	binary AND
^	binary exclusive OR
|	binary OR
&&	logical AND
||	logical OR
()	parenthesized expression for grouping. Necessary if the expression contains <, >, &, or |.
{cmd}	1 if *cmd* terminates with 0 exit status; 0 otherwise.

Expression operators may also include logical file enquiries of the form *-l name* where *l* is one of:

d	directory
e	existence
f	plain file
o	ownership
r	read access
w	write access
x	execute access
z	zero size

and *name* is command and filename expanded before the test is performed.

History Event Selection

!!	re-execute last command
!*n*	re-execute command *n* from history list
!*pattern*	re-execute most recent command from the history list that begins with *pattern*
!?*pattern*?	re-execute most recent command from the history list that contains *pattern*

Word Specifications

Within history substitutions it is possible to select individual words in the command to supply or to modify the previous command. Follow event by a colon ":" to access the following words except where it is stated that the colon may be omitted.

0	first word (command name) e.g. !!:0
n	(*n*+1)th word e.g. !!:3
^	second word (first argument) (colon may be omitted) e.g. !!^
$	last word (colon may be omitted) e.g. !!$
%	match the word of the immediately preceding ?*pattern*? (colon may be omitted)
x-y	range of arguments from *x* through *y* e.g. !!:5-7
-*y*	abbreviates '0-*y*' (colon may be omitted)
*	stands for ^$ (colon may be omitted)
*x**	abbreviate *x*–$ where *x* is position number
x-	like x* but omitting last word

History Modifiers

Follow event or **optional** word designations with a modifier below to perform the following functions:

:e	remove all but the extension .xxx e.g. !!:3:e
:h	remove trailing pathname leaving the head e.g. !!$:h
:p	command is printed but not executed e.g. !!*:p
:r	remove trailing .xxx leaving root name e.g. !!$:r
:s/*old*/*new*	substitute new contents for old contents e.g. !!:s/tim/jim/ To substitute string in immediately preceding command, you may use ^, e.g. !!:s/tim/jim/ = ^tim^jim.
:q	quote the substituted values and prevent further substitutions e.g. !!:s/jim/sim/:q
:t	remove leading pathname leaving tail e.g. !!:3:t
:x	divide words at blanks, tabs, and newlines e.g. !!:x
:&	repeat previous substitution e.g. !6:&
:g	change globally e.g. !!:g:s/tim/jim/

alias [*name*] [*cmd*]

Assign *name* as the alias for *cmd*. If *cmd* is not specified, print the alias for *name*; if *name* also is not specified, print all aliases.

alias

---

bg [*%job* ...]

Put the current or the specified jobs into background. Same as *%jobn* &.

bg

---

break

Resume execution after end of nearest enclosing **while** or **foreach**.

break

---

breaksw

Cause break from a switch: continue execution after **endsw**.

breaksw

---

case *pattern*

Identify a *pattern* in a **switch**.

case

---

cd [*dir*]

Change working directory to *dir*; default is home directory of user.

cd

---

chdir	**chdir** [*dir*] Same as **cd**.
continue	**continue** Continue execution of nearest enclosing **while** or **foreach**.
default	**default** Label the default case in a **switch**.
dirs	**dirs** Print the directory stack.
echo	**echo** [**-n**] string Write *string* to standard output; if **-n** is specified, the output is not terminated by a newline.
eval	**eval** *arg* ... Evaluate arguments as a command line and use the result as input to the shell.
exec	**exec** *command* Execute *command* in place of current shell.

exit [(*expr*)]

Exit shell with status value of last command or value specified by *expr*.

exit

---

fg [*%job* ...]

Bring current or specified job to the foreground. Same as *%jobn.*

fg

---

foreach *name* (*wordlist*)
    commands
end

Set variable name to each member of *wordlist* and execute *commands* between **foreach** and **end**.

foreach

---

glob *wordlist*

Like **echo**, but no ''\'' escapes are recognized, and words are delimited by null characters.

glob

---

goto *string*

Continue execution following the next occurrence of *string* followed by a **:**, which may be preceded by blanks and tabs but otherwise must be alone on the line.

goto

---

hashstat

Print the statistics for the effectiveness of the internal hash table used for locating commands in path.

hashstat

---

history	**history**
	Display the list of history events. (History syntax is discussed earlier in this section.)
if	**if** (*expression*) *command*
	or **if** (*expr1*) **then**
	commands1
	[**else if** (*expr2*) **then**
	commands2]
	&#8942;
	else
	commands3
	endif
	If *expression* is true, do *command*.
	Or if *expr1* is true, then execute *commands1*; else if *expr2* is true, then execute *commands2*; if neither is true, execute *commands3*.
jobs	**jobs** [-l]
	List of active jobs; if -l is specified, process ids are printed as well.
kill	**kill** [-*sig*] *pid*
	Terminate the designated process (*pid*) optionally with a signal (*sig*). **kill** -l will list available signal names.
limit	**limit** *resource maximum-use*
	Limit the consumption by the current process and each process it creates to not individually exceed *maximum-use* on the specified *resource*. If no *maximum-use* is given, then the current limit is printed; if no *resource* is given, then all limitations are

given. Resources include **cputime, filesize, datasize, stacksize,** and **coredumpsize.**	**limit** *continued*

login Replace login shell with **/bin/login.**	**login**

logout Terminate login shell.	**logout**

newgrp *group* Change the group id of the caller. A new shell is executed and the current shell state is lost.	**newgrp**

nice [+*number*] command Schedule a command to be performed at a low priority where *number* is the priority number and *command* is the command to be performed; default number is 4.	**nice**

nohup [*command*] Do not terminate command if terminal line is closed. Use without command in shell scripts to keep script from being terminated.	**nohup**

notify [*%job* ...] Causes shell to report a change of status for the current or specified jobs.	**notify**

onintr	**onintr** [-] [*label*] Restore the default action of shell on interrupts. With the - option, ignore all interrupts; with *label*, cause the shell to execute a "**goto** *label*" when an interrupt is received.
popd	**popd** +*n* Pop the directory stack and return to the new top directory; +*n* discards the *n*th entry in the stack.
pushd	**pushd** [*name*] or **pushd** +*n* Change to *name* directory and add current directory to the stack. With no *name* specified, exchange the top two elements of the directory stack. Or change to *n*th directory and put it on top of the stack.
rehash	**rehash** Recompute hash table for *path*. Use whenever a new command is added to path during the current session.
repeat	**repeat** *n command* Execute *n* instances of *command*.
set	**set** [*variable* [*n*] [=*value* . . .]] Set *variable* to *value*, or if multiple values are specified, set the variable to the list of words in the value list. If an index *n* is specified, set the *n*th word in the variable to *value*. (The variable must already

contain at least that number of words.) With no arguments, display value of all set variables.	**set** *continued*

setenv *name value* Set the value of *name* to be *value* (a single string). **setenv** is not necessary for the **USER, TERM** and **PATH** variables.	**setenv**

shift [*array*] Shift positional arguments in specified *array*; e.g. **$2** becomes **$1**.	**shift**

source *file* Read commands from *file*.	**source**

stop [*%job* ...] Stop the current or specified job executing in background.	**stop**

suspend Stop the shell, as if it were sent a **stop** signal with **$$**.	**suspend**

switch *(string)*
case *pattern1*:
    commands
[**breaksw**]
case *pattern2*:
    commands
    ⋮
	switch
	
	☞

switch *continued*	[breaksw] **default:** *commands* [breaksw] **endsw** Match each case *pattern* against the specified *string*. Execute commands following each pattern that matches, or after **default:** if no pattern matches. Use **breaksw** to break out of the switch once a match has been made.
time	**time** [*command*] Display a summary of time used by *command* or by the shell if no arguments are specified.
umask	**umask** [*nnn*] Display file creation mask or set file creation mask to octal *nnn*. The file creation mask determines which permission bits are turned off; e.g., **umask 002** produces **rw-rw-r--**.
unalias	**unalias** *name* Remove *name* from the alias list. See **alias**.
unhash	**unhash** Remove internal hash table.
unlimit	**unlimit** [*resource*] Remove the limitations on *resource*. If *resource* is not specified, remove limitations on all resources. See **limit**.

unset *pattern*	**unset**
Remove variables that match specified *pattern* (filename metacharacters may be used in *pattern*).	
unsetenv *name*	**unsetenv**
Remove environment variables that match specified *name* (filename metacharacters may be used in *name*).	
wait	**wait**
Wait for all background jobs to terminate.	
while *(expression)* ... *commands* **end**	**while**
While the *expression* evaluates non-zero, evaluate *commands* between **while** and **end**. **break** and **continue** can be used to terminate or continue the loop.	
@ [*variable* [*n*] = *expression*]	**@**
Assign the value of the arithmetic *expression* to *variable*, or to the *n*th element of *variable* if the index *n* is specified. Expression operators are listed earlier in this section. With no variable or expression specified, print the values of all shell variables. The special formats **@** *variable++* and **@** *variable--* will increment and decrement *variable* by one, respectively.	

The Bourne Shell vs. The C Shell

Function	csh	sh
Prompt	%	#
Begin program	#	:
Redirect output	>	>
Force output	>!	
Append to file	>>	>>
Force append	>>!	
Redirect input	<	<
"Here" document	<<	<<
Combine stdout and stderr	>&	2>&1
Read from terminal	$<	read
Pipe output	|	|
Obsolete pipe		^
Run process in background	&	&
Separate commands on same line	;	;
Match any character(s) in filename	*	*
Match single character in filename	?	?
Match any characters enclosed	[]	[]
Execute in subshell	( )	( )
Match each element in enclosed list	{ }	{ }
Substitute output of enclosed command	` `	` `
Partial quote (allows variable and command expansion)	" "	" "
Full quote	' '	' '
Quote following character	\	\
Begin comment	#	:
Home directory	$home	$HOME
Assign value to variable	set	=
Use value for variable	$var	$var
Process id	$$	$$
Command name	$0	$0
nth argument (0<n<9)	$n	$n
All arguments as a simple "word"	$*	$*
All arguments as separate "words"		$@
Number of arguments	$#argv or $#	$#
Exit status	$status	$?
Background exit status		$!
Current options		$-
Interpret file	**source**	.

3

Pattern Matching

A number of UNIX text processing programs, including *ed*, *ex*, *vi*, *sed, awk,* and *grep*, allow you to perform searches, and in some cases make changes, by searching for text patterns rather than fixed strings. These text patterns (also called regular expressions) are made up by combining normal characters with a number of special characters.

Metacharacters

The special characters and their use are listed below:

.   Matches any *single* character except *newline*.

*   Matches any number (including zero) of the single character (including a character specified by a regular expression) that immediately precedes it. For example, since "." (dot) means any character, ".*" means "match any number of characters".

[...]   Matches any *one* of the characters enclosed between the brackets. For example, "[AB]" matches either "A" or "B". A range of consecutive characters can be specified by separating the first and last characters in the range with a hyphen. For example, "[A-Z]" will match any upper case letter from "A" to "Z" and "[0-9]" will match any digit from "0" to "9". Some metachararacters lose special meaning inside brackets. A circumflex (∧) as the first character in the bracket reverses the sense: it tries to match any one character *not* in the list.

\{*n,m*\} Matches a range of occurrences of the single character (including a character specified by a regular expression) that immediately precedes it. *n* and *m* are integers between 0 and 256 that specify how many occurrences to match. \{*n*\} will match exactly *n* occurrences, \{*n,*\} will match at least *n* occurrences, and \{*n,m*\} will match any number of occurrences between *n* and *m*. For example, "A\{2,3\}" will match either "AA" (as in "AARDVARK") or "AAA" (as in "AAA Travel Agency") but will not match the single letter "A".

∧   Requires that the following regular expression be found at the beginning of the line.

$ Requires that the preceding regular expression be found at the end of the line.

\   Treats the following special character as an ordinary character. For example, "\." stands for a period and "*" for an asterisk.

\(\)   Saves the pattern enclosed between "\(" and "\)" into a special holding space. Up to nine patterns can be saved in this way on a single line. They can be "replayed" in substitutions by the escape sequences "\1" to "\9". Not used in **grep** and **egrep**.

n   Matches the *n*th pattern previously saved by "\(" and "\)", where *n* is a number from 0 to 9 and previously saved patterns are counted from the left on the line. Not used in **grep** and **egrep**.

&	Prints the entire search pattern when used in a replacement string.

egrep and awk use an extended set of metacharacters:

regexp +	Matches one or more occurrences of the regular expression.
regexp ?	Matches 0 or 1 occurrences of the regular expression.
regexp | *regexp*	Matches lines containing either *regexp*.
(*regexp*)	Used for grouping.

ex regular expressions (: commands from **vi**) offer an extended set of metacharacters:

\<	Matches characters at beginning (\<) or at the end (\>) of
\>	a word. The expression "\<ac" would only match words which began with "ac," such as "action" but not "react."
\u	Convert first character of replacement string to uppercase.
\U	Convert replacement string to uppercase.
\l	Convert first character of replacement string to lowercase.
\L	Convert replacement string to lowercase.

Pattern Matching Examples

For example, you can use patterns in the following **vi** and **ex** commands:

/*pattern*	Search for *pattern*.
?*pattern*	Search backwards for *pattern*.
:**d**/*pattern*/	Deletes from the cursor position up to *pattern*.
:**s**/*pattern*/*replacement*/	Substitute *replacement* for *pattern*.
:**g**/*pattern*/*command*	Globally perform *command* on every line containing *pattern*.
:%**s**/*pattern*/*replacement*/**g**	Globally substitute *replacement* for *pattern*.
:/*pattern1*/,/*pattern2*/**d**	Delete the lines between *pattern1* and *pattern2*, inclusive.
:/*pattern1*/,/*pattern2*/**co** *line*	Copy the lines between *pattern1* and *pattern2*, inclusive, to *line*.
:/*pattern1*/,/*pattern2*/**mo** *line*	Move the lines between *pattern1* and *pattern2*, inclusive, to *line*.

You can use patterns in the following **sed** commands:

/*pattern*/**a**\ *text*	Insert *text* on the line(s) following *pattern*.
/*pattern*/**i**\ *text*	Insert *text* on the line before *pattern*.
/*pattern*/**c**\ *text*	Change the line addressed by *pattern* to *text*.
s/*pattern*/*replacement*/	Substitute *replacement* for *pattern*.
/*pattern*/**d**	Delete lines containing *pattern*.

4

Editor Command Summary

This section is divided into four major parts:

- The **vi** editor.
- The **ex** editor.
- The **sed** editor.
- The **awk** data manipulation language.

The vi Editor

Review of vi Operations

Entering vi

$ vi [+n|+/pattern/] [file]

Open *file* for editing, optionally at line *n* or at the first line matching *pattern*. If no file is specified, open *vi* with an empty buffer. See Section 1 for more information on command-line options for *vi*.

Command Mode

Once the file is opened, you are in command mode. From command mode, you can invoke insert mode, issue editing commands, move the cursor to a different position in the file, invoke *ex* commands or a UNIX shell, and save or exit the current version of the file.

Insert Mode

The following commands invoke insert mode:

a A i I o O R s S

While in insert mode, you can enter new text in the file. Press the ESCAPE key to exit insert mode and return to command mode.

Command Syntax

The syntax for editing commands is:

[*n*] *operator* [*m*] *object*

The commands that position the cursor in the file represent objects which the basic editing operators can take as arguments. Objects represent all characters up to (or back to) the designated object. The cursor movement keys and pattern matching commands can be used as objects.

The basic editing operators are:

c   For change

d   For delete

y   For yank or copy

If the current line is the object of the operation, then the operator is the same as the object: **cc, dd, yy.** *n* and *m* are the number of times the operation is performed or the number of objects the operation is performed on. If both *n* and *m* are specified, the effect is $n \times m$.

The following text objects are represented:

word	Includes characters up to a space or punctuation mark. Capitalized object is variant form which recognizes only blank spaces.
sentence	Is up to . ! ? followed by two spaces.
paragraph	Is up to next blank line or paragraph macro defined by **para=** option.
section	Is up to next section heading defined by **sect=** option.

Examples:

2cw	Change the next two words
d}	Delete up to next paragraph
d^	Delete back to beginning of line
5yy	Copy the next five lines
3dl	Delete three characters right of cursor

Status Line Commands

Most commands are not echoed on the screen as you input them. However, the status line at the bottom of the screen is used to echo input for the following commands:

/ ?	For pattern matching search
:	Invoke an *ex* command
!	Invoke a UNIX command that takes as its input an object in the buffer and replaces it with output from the command.

Commands that are input on the status line must be entered by pressing the RETURN key. In addition, error messages and output from the **^G** command are displayed on the status line.

For more information on *vi*, refer to the Nutshell Handbook, *Learning the vi Editor*.

Saving and Exiting

ZZ	Quit *vi*, saving changes
:wq	Quit *vi*, saving changes
:q!	Force quit and ignore changes
:w	Save changes and stay in file
:w *file*	Save copy to *file*
:f *file*	Change current filename to *file*
:w %.old	Use current filename to save as *file.old*
:*nl*,*n2***w** *file*	Write line *nl* to *n2* to *file*
:w!	Force overwrite of existing file

Editing Multiple Files

:e *file*	Edit another *file*; current file becomes alternate
:e!	Restore last saved version of current file
:e + *file*	Begin editing at end of *file*
:e +*n file*	Open *file* at line *n*
:e #	Open to previous position in alternate file
:ta *tag*	Edit file at location *tag*
:n	Edit next file
:n!	Forces next file
:n *files*	Specify new list of *files*
^G	Show current file and line number
:args	Display multiple files to be edited
:rew	Rewind list of multiple files to top

Inserting New Text

a	Insert after cursor
A	Append to end of line
i	Insert before cursor
I	Insert at beginning of line
o	Insert one line below cursor
O	Insert one line above cursor
ESC	Terminate insert mode
^J	Move down one line
^W	Move back one word
RETURN	Add a newline
BACKSPACE	Move back one character
KILL	Delete current line (set with **stty**)
^H	Move back one character
^I	Insert a tab
^T	Move to next tab setting
^V	Quote next character

Positioning the Cursor

A number preceding a command repeats movement. Commands are also objects for change, delete and yank operations.

By Character or Line

h or ←	Left one character
j or ↓	Down one line
k or ↑	Up one line
l or →	Right one line
^	To first character of current line
0	To first position of current line
$	To end of current line
SPACE	Right one character
RETURN	First character of next line
+	First character of next line
-	First character of previous line
G	To last line in file
nG	To line number n
:n	To line number n
H	Home - top line on screen
M	Middle line on screen
L	Last line on screen
nH	To n lines after top line
nL	To n lines before last line

By Word

b	Back one word
B	Back one word (ignore punctuation)
e	End of next word
E	End of next word (ignore punctuation)
w	Start of next word
W	Start of next word (ignore punctuation)

By Sentence or Paragraph

(	Beginning of previous sentence
)	Beginning of next sentence
G	End of file
[[	Back one section
]]	Forward one section
{	Beginning of previous paragraph
}	Beginning of next paragraph

Scrolling the Screen

^B	Scroll back one screen
^F	Forward one screen
^D	Scroll forward half screen
^U	Scroll back half screen
^L	Clear and redraw screen
^R	Refresh screen
^E	Scroll up one line
^Y	Scroll down one line

Changing and Deleting Text

cw	Change word
cc	Change line
C	Change text from current position to end of line
3cl	Change three characters right of cursor
dd	Delete current line
*n*dd	Delete *n* lines
D	Delete remainder of line
dw	Delete a word
d}	Delete up to next paragraph
d^	Delete back to beginning of line
4dh	Delete four characters left of cursor
d/*pat*	Delete up to first occurrence of pattern
dn	Delete up to next occurrence of pattern
df*a*	Delete up to and including *a* on current line
dt*a*	Delete up to (not including) *a* on current line
dL	Delete up to last line on screen
dG	Delete to end of file
p	Insert last deleted text after cursor
P	Insert last deleted text before cursor
r*x*	Replace character with *x*
R*text*	Replace text beginning at cursor
s	Substitute character
S	Substitute entire line
u	Undo last change
U	Restore current line
x	Delete current cursor position
X	Delete back one character
.	Repeat last change
~	Reverse case

Searching

/text	Search forward for *text*
n	Repeat previous search
N	Repeat search in opposite direction
/	Repeat forward search
?	Repeat previous search backward
?*text*	Search backward for *text*
/text/+n	Go to line *n* after */text*
?*text*?*-n*	Go to line *n* before */text*
%	Find match of current parenthesis, brace, or bracket
f*x*	Move ahead to *x* on current line
F*x*	Move back to *x* on current line
t*c*	Search forward before *c* in current line
T*c*	Search back after *c* in current line
,	Reverse search direction of last **f**, **F**, **t**, or **T**.
;	Repeat last character search (**f**, **F**, **t**, or **T**)

Copying and Moving

Y or yy	Copy current line to new buffer
"*x***yy**	Yank current line to buffer *x*
"*x***d**	Delete into buffer *x*
"*x***p**	Put contents of buffer *x*
yy	Copy current line
y]]	Copy up to next section heading
ye	Copy to end of word

Marking and Returning

m*x*	Mark current position with *x*
´*x*	Move cursor to *x*
`*x*	Move cursor to *x* of current line
´´	Return to previous mark or context after move

Interacting With UNIX

:r *file*	Read in contents of *file* after cursor
:r !*cmd*	Read in output from command after cursor
:*nr* !*cmd*	Read in output from command after line *n* (0 for top of file).
:!*cmd*	Run command then return
!*obj cmd*	Send object in buffer to UNIX command and replace with output
:*n1,n2*! *cmd*	Send lines *n1* through *n2* to command and replace with output
n!!**cmd**	Send *n* lines to UNIX command and replace with output
!!	Repeat last system command
:sh	Create subshell; return to file with ^D
^?	Interrupt editor, resume with **fg** (not available in all versions).
^Z	Interrupt editor, resume with **fg** (not available in all versions).
:so *file*	Read and execute commands from *file*

Macros

:ab *in out*	Use *in* as abbreviation for *out*
:unab *in*	Remove abbreviation
:ab	List abbreviations
:map *c seq*	Map character *c* as sequence of commands
:unmap *c*	Disable map for character *c*
:map! *c seq*	Map character *c* to input mode sequence
:unmap! *c*	Disable input mode map
:map	List characters that are mapped

Miscellaneous Commands

^Q	Quote next character
<<	Shift lines left one shift width (default 8 spaces)
>>	Shift lines right one shift width (default 8 spaces)

The vi Editor

a   Append text after cursor.
A   Append text at end of line.
^A   Unused.

b   Back up to beginning of word in current line.
B   Back up to word, ignoring punctuation.
^B   Scroll backward one window.

c   Change operator.
C   Change to end of current line.
^C   Unused.

d   Delete operator.
D   Delete to end of current line.
^D   Scroll down half-window.

e   Move to end of word.
E   Move to end of word, ignoring punctuation.
^E   Show one more line at bottom of window.

f   Find next character typed forward on current line.
F   Find next character typed back on current line.
^F   Scroll Forward one window.

g   Unused.
G   Go to specified line or end of file.
^G   Print information about file on status line.

h   Left arrow cursor key.
H   Move cursor to Home position.
^H   Left arrow cursor key; backspace key in insert mode.

i   Insert text before cursor.
I   Insert text at beginning of line.
^I   Unused in command mode; in insert mode is same as TAB key.

j   Down arrow cursor key.
J   Join two lines.
^J   Down arrow cursor key.

k   Up arrow cursor key.
K   Unused.
^K   Unused.

l   Right arrow cursor key.
L   Move cursor to Last position in window.
^L   Redraw screen.

m   Mark the current cursor position in register (a-z).
M   Move cursor to Middle position in window.
^M   Carriage return.

Editors

n	Repeat the last search command.
N	Repeat the last search command in reverse direction.
^N	Down arrow cursor key.
o	Open line below current line.
O	Open line above current line.
^O	Unused.
p	Put yanked or deleted text after or below cursor.
P	Put yanked or deleted text before or above cursor.
^P	Up arrow cursor key.
q	Unused.
Q	Quit *vi* and invoke *ex*.
^Q	Unused in command mode; in input mode, quote next character.
r	Replace character at cursor with the next character you type.
R	Replace characters.
^R	Redraw the screen.
s	Change the character under the cursor to typed characters.
S	Change entire line.
^S	Unused.
t	Move cursor forward to character before next character typed.
T	Move cursor back to character after next character typed.
^T	Unused in command mode; in insert mode, used with *autoindent* option set.
u	Undo the last change made.
U	Restore current line, discarding changes.
^U	Scroll the screen upward half-window.
v	Unused.
V	Unused.
^V	Unused in command mode; in insert mode, quote next character.
w	Move to beginning of next word.
W	Move to beginning of next word, ignoring punctuation.
^W	Unused in command mode; in insert mode, back up to beginning of word.
x	Delete character under the cursor.
X	Delete character before cursor.
^X	Unused.
y	Yank or copy operator.
Y	Make copy of current line.
^Y	Show one more line at top of window.
z	Redraw the screen, repositioning cursor when followed by RETURN at the top, . at the middle, and - at the bottom of screen.
ZZ	Exit the editor, saving changes.
^Z	Unused.

The following characters are unused in command mode and can be mapped as user-defined commands.

^A	^C	g	^I
K	^K	^O	q
^Q	^S	^T	v
V	^V	^W	^X
^Z			

vi and ex Options

Options allow you to change characteristics of the editing environment.

Options may be put in the **.exrc** file or set during a *vi* session, using the **set** command:

:set *x*	Enable option
:set no*x*	Disable option
:set *x=val*	Give value *val*
:set	Show changed options
:set all	Show all options
:set *x*?	Show value of option *x*

(The colon should not be typed if the command is put in **.exrc**)

Available Options

The following options can be specified with the **set** command:

autoindent	Supply indent
autoprint	Display changes after each editor command
autowrite	Write before changing files
beautify	Ignores control characters during input
directory	Directory to store buffer file
edcompatible	Uses *ed* features
errorbells	Error messages ring bell
hardtabs	Sets terminal hardware tabs
ignorecase	Scan without regard to U/L case
lisp	Insert indents in lisp format
list	Print ^I for tab, $ at end
magic	. [* special in patterns
mesg	Permit messages to terminal
number	Display line numbers
open	Allow entry to *open* or *visual* mode
optimize	Abolish carriage returns when printing multiple lines
paragraphs	Macros for paragraphs
prompt	Set *ex* prompt
readonly	No write without !
redraw	Simulate smart terminal
remap	Retains nested map sequences
report	Specifies size for reporting changes
scroll	Amount of lines to scroll
sections	Provide macro names for sections
shell	Pathname for shell escape
shiftwidth	Set width of software tabstop
showmatch	When "(" or "{" is typed move cursor to next match of ")" or "}"
showmode	Print "input mode" when input mode is entered
tabstop	Set number of spaces indented by a tab

taglength	Significant characters in tag
tags	Path of files for functions
term	Terminal type
terse	Brief error messages
timeout	Macros "time out" after one second
ttytype	Terminal type
warn	"No write since last change"
window	Show a certain number of lines on screen
wrapscan	Search past end of file
wrapmargin	Define right margin
writeany	Allows to save any file

Editors

The ex Editor

ex is a line editor that serves as the foundation for the screen editor, *vi*. *ex* commands work on the current line or a range of lines in a file. In *vi*, *ex* commands are preceded by a colon and entered by pressing RETURN. You can also invoke *ex* on its own just as you invoke *vi* or as you enter *ex* from *vi*.

The *vi* command "Q" can be used to quit the *vi* editor and enter *ex*.

To exit *ex*:
>   **:x**   To exit, saving changes
>   **:q!**   To quit, without saving changes

The *ex* command ":vi" can be used to quit *ex* and enter the *vi* editor.

To enter an *ex* command from *vi*:

>   :[*address*] *command* [*options*]

An initial : indicates an ex command. The *address* is the line number or range of lines that are the object of the *command*.

Options:
>   **!**   Indicates a variant form of the command.
>   *parameters*
>   Indicates that additional information can be supplied. A parameter can be the name of a file.
>   *count*   The number of times the command is to be repeated.
>   *flag*   "#", "p" and "l" indicate print format.

Unlike *vi* commands, the count cannot precede the command as it will be taken for the address. "**d3**" deletes three lines beginning with current line; "**3d**" deletes line 3. As you type the address and command, it is echoed on the status line. Enter the command by pressing the RETURN key.

Addresses

If no address is given, the current line is the object of the command. If the addresses specifies a range of lines, the format is:

>   *x,y*

where *x* and *y* are the first and last addressed lines (*x* must precede *y* in buffer). *x* and *y* may be a line number or a primitive. Using ";" instead of "," sets the current line to *x* before interpreting *y*.

1,$ addresses all lines in the file.

Address Symbols

.	Current line
n	Absolute line number
$	Last line
%	All lines, same as **"1,$"**
x-|+*n*	*n* lines before or after *x*
-[*n*]	One or *n* lines previous
+[*n*]	One or *n* lines ahead
´*x*	Line marked with *x*
´´	Previous context
/*pat*/ or ?*pat*?	Ahead or back to line matching *pat*

See Section 3 for more information on using patterns.

abbrev	**ab** [*string text*] Define *string* when typed to be translated into *text*. If *string* and *text* are not specified, list all current abbreviations.
append	[*address*] **a**[!] *text* . Append *text* at specified *address*, or at present address if none is specified. With the ! flag, toggle the **autoindent** setting during the input of *text*.
args	**ar** Print the members of the argument list, with the current argument printed within brackets ([ ]).
change	[*address*] **c**[!] *text* . Replace the specified lines with *text*. With the ! flag, toggle the **autoindent** setting during the input of *text*.
copy	[*address*] **co** *destination* Copy the lines included in *address* to the specified *destination* address. The command **t** is a synonym for **copy**.

[*address*] **d** [*buffer*]	**delete**

Delete the lines included in *address*. If *buffer* is specified, save or append the text to the named buffer.

e[!] [*+n*] *file*	**edit**

Begin editing on *file*. If the ! flag is used, do not warn if the present file has not been saved since the last change. If the *+n* argument is used, begin editing on line *n*.

f [*filename*]	**file**

Change the name of the current file to *filename*, which is considered "not edited". If no *filename* is specified, print the current status of the file.

[*address*] **g**[!]/*pattern*/[*commands*]	**global**

Execute *commands* on all lines which contain *pattern*, or if *address* is specified, all lines within that range. If *commands* are not specified, print all such lines. If the ! flag is used, execute *commands* on all lines *not* containing *pattern*.

[*address*] **i**[!] *text*	**insert**

.

Insert *text* at line before the specified address, or at present address if none is specified. With the ! flag, toggle the **autoindent** setting during the input of *text*.

Editor Command Summary 4-17

join	[*address*] **j** [*count*] Place the text in the specified range on one line, with white space adjusted to provide two blank characters after a ".", no blank characters if a ")" follows, and one blank character otherwise.
k	[*address*] **k** *char* Mark the given *address* with *char*. Return later to the line with **'x**.
list	[*address*] **l** [*count*] Print the specified lines in an unambiguous manner.
map	**map** *char commands* Define a macro named *char* in visual mode with the specified sequence of commands. *char* may be a single character, or the sequence *#n*, representing a function key on the keyboard.
mark	[*address*] **ma** *char* Mark the specified line with *char*, a single lower-case letter. Return later to the line with **'x**.
move	[*address*] **m** *destination* Move the lines specified by *address* to the *destination* address.

n[!] [[+*command*] *filelist*]   **next**

Edit the next file in the command line argument list.
Use **args** for a listing of arguments. If *filelist* is provided, replace the current argument list with *filelist*
and begin editing on the first file; if *command* is
given (containing no spaces), execute *command* after
editing the first such file.

[*address*] nu [*count*]   **number**

Print each line specified by *address* preceded by its
buffer line number. **#** may be used as an abbreviation
for **number** as well as **nu**.

[*address*] o [/*pattern*/]   **open**

Enter *open* mode at the lines specified by *address*, or
lines matching *pattern*. Exit open mode with **Q**.

---

pre   **preserve**

Save the current editor buffer as though the system
had crashed.

[*address*] p [*count*]   **print**

Print the lines specified by *address* with non-printing
characters printed. **P** may also be used as an abbreviation.

[*address*] pu [*char*]   **put**

Restore previously deleted or yanked lines from
named buffer specified by *char* to the line specified
by *address*; if *char* is not specified, the last deleted or
yanked text is restored.

---

quit	**q[!]** Terminate current editing session. If the file was not saved since the last change, or if there are files in the argument list that have not yet be accessed, you will not be able to quit without the **!** flag.
read	*[address]* **r[!]** *file* Copy the text of *file* at the specified *address*. If *file* is not specified, the current filename is used.
read	*[address]* **r** *!command* Read in the output of *command* into the text after the line specified by *address*.
recover	**rec** *[file]* Recover *file* from system save area.
rewind	**rew[!]** Rewind argument list and begin editing the first file in the list. The **!** flag rewinds without warning if file has not been saved since the last change.
set	**se** *parameter parameter2* ... Set a value to an option with each *parameter*, or if no *parameter* is supplied, print all options that have been changed from their defaults. For Boolean-valued options, each *parameter* can be phrased as "*option*" or "**no***option*"; other options can be assigned with the syntax, "*option=value*"

sh	**shell**

Create a new shell. Resume editing when the shell is terminated.

---

so *file*	**source**

Read and execute commands from *file*.

[*address*] **s** [*/pattern/repl/*] [*options*] [*count*]	**substitute**

Replace each instance of *pattern* on the specified lines with *repl*. If *pattern* and *repl* are omitted, repeat last substitution.

options

   g   Substitute all instances of *pattern*.
   c   Prompt for confirmation before each change.

[*address*] **t** *destination*	**t**

Copy the lines included in *address* to the specified *destination* address.

[*address*] **ta** *tag*	**ta**

Switch the focus of editing to *tag*.

---

una *word*	**unabbreviate**

Remove *word* from the list of abbreviations.

---

undo	**u**
	Reverse the changes made by the last editing command.
unmap	**unm** *char*
	Remove *char* from the list of macros.
v	[*address*] **v**/*pattern*/[*commands*]
	Execute *commands* on all lines *not* containing *pattern*. If *commands* are not specified, print all such lines.
version	**ve**
	Print the current version number of the editor and the date the editor was last changed.
visual	[*address*] **vi** [*type*] [*count*]
	Enter visual mode at the line specified by *address*. Exit with **Q**.
	type
	-, ^, or . (See the **z** command).
	count
	Specify an initial window size.
visual	*vi* [+*n*] *file*
	Begin editing on *file* in visual mode.

[address] **w**[!] [[>>] *file]*	**write**

Write lines specified by *address* to *file*, or full contents of buffer if *address* is not specified. If *file* is also omitted, save the contents of the buffer to the current filename. If >> *file* is used, write contents to the end of the specified *file*. The ! flag forces the editor to write over any current contents of *file*.

[address] **w** !*command*	**write**

Write lines specified by *address* to *command*.

wq[!]	**wq**

Write and quit the file in one movement.

x	**xit**

Write file if changes have been made to the buffer since last write, then quit.

[address] **ya** *[char]* *[count]*	**yank**

Place lines specified by *address* in named buffer indicated by *char*, or if no *char* is specified place in general buffer.

[address] **z** *[type]* *[count]*	**z**

Print a window of text with line specified by *address* at the top.

type

    +   place specified line at the top of the window (default).

☞

z *continued*	- place specified line at bottom of the window. . place specified line in the center of the window. ^ print the window before the window associated with type -. = place specified line in the center of the window and leave the current line at this line. *count* Specifies the number of lines to be displayed.
!	[*address*] !*command* Execute *command* in a shell. If *address* is specified, apply the lines contained in *address* as standard input to *command*, and replace the lines with the output.
=	[*address*] = Print the line number of the line indicated by *address*.
< >	[*address*] < [*count*] or [*address*] > [*count*] Shift lines specified by *address* in specified direction. Only blanks and tabs are shifted in a left-shift (<).
address	*address* Print the lines specified in *address*.
RETURN	*RETURN* Print the next line in the file.

[address] & *[options]* *[count]*

Repeat the previous substitute command.

&

[address] ~ *[count]*

Replace the previous regular expression with the previous replacement pattern from a **substitute** command.

~

The sed Editor

sed [*options*] *file(s)*

The following options are recognized:

-n   only print lines specified with the **p** command, or the **p** flag of the **s**
            command
-e *cmd*   next argument is an editing command
-f *file*   next argument is a file containing editing commands

sed commands have the general form:

[*address*][,*address*][!]*command* [*arguments*]

sed copies each line of input into a pattern space. **sed** instructions consist of
addresses and editing commands. If the address of the command matches the
line in the pattern space, then the command is applied to that line. If a command has no address, then it is applied to each input line. It is important to note
that a command affects the contents of the space; subsequent command
addresses attempt to match the line in the pattern space, not the original input
line.

Pattern Addressing

An *address* can either be a line number or a *pattern*, enclosed in slashes (*/pat-
tern/*). Patterns can make use of regular expressions, as described in Section 3.
Additionally, "\n" can be used to match any newline in the pattern space (resulting from the N command), but not the newline at the end of the pattern
space. If no pattern is specified, *command* will be applied to all lines. If only
one address is specified, the command will be applied to all lines between the
first and second addresses, inclusively. Some commands can only accept one
address.

The ! operator following a pattern causes **sed** to apply the command to all lines
that do not contain the pattern.

A series of commands can be grouped after one pattern by enclosing the command list in curly braces:

[*/pattern/*][,*/pattern/*]{
command1
command2
}

:*label*   :

Specify a label to be branched to by **b** or **t**. *label* may contain up to eight characters.

[/*pattern*/]=   =

Write to standard output the line number of each line addressed by *pattern*.

[*address*]a\   a
text

Append *text* following each line matched by *address*. If *text* goes over more than one line, newlines must be "hidden" by preceding them with a backslash. The insertion will be terminated by the first newline that is not hidden in this way. The results of this command are read into the pattern space (creating a multi-line pattern space) and sent to standard output when the list of editing commands is finished or a command explicitly prints the pattern space.

[*address1*][,*address2*]b[*label*]   b

Branch to *label* placed with : command, or if no *label*, to the end of the script. That is, *skip* all subsequent editing commands (up to *label*) for each addressed line.

[*address1*][,*address2*]c\   c
text

Replace pattern space with *text*. (See **a** for details on *text*.)

---

d	[*address1*][,*address2*]**d** Delete line in pattern space. Thus, line is not passed to standard output and a new line of input is read; editing resumes with first command in list.
D	[*address1*][*address2*]**D** Delete first part (up to embedded newline) of multi-line pattern created by **N** command and begin editing. Same as **d** if **N** has not been applied to a line.
g	[*address1*][,*address2*]**g** Copy contents of hold space (see **h** or **H** command) into pattern space, wiping out previous contents.
G	[*address1*][,*address2*]**G** Append contents of hold space (see **h** or **H** command) to contents of the pattern space.
h	[*address1*][,*address2*]**h** Copy pattern space into hold space, a special buffer. Previous contents of hold space are obliterated.
H	[*address1*][,*address2*]**H** Append pattern space to contents of the hold space. Previous and new contents are separated by a newline.

[*address1*]**i**\
text

Insert *text* before each line matched by *address*. (See
a for details on *text*.)

[*address1*][,*address2*]**l**

List the contents of the pattern space, showing non-
printing characters as ASCII codes. Long lines are
wrapped.

[*address1*][,*address2*]**n**

Read next line of input into pattern space. Current
line is output but control passes to next editing command instead of beginning at top of list.

[*address1*][,*address2*]**N**

Append next input line to contents of pattern space;
the two lines are separated by an embedded newline.
(This command is designed to allow pattern matches
across two lines.)

[*address1*][,*address2*]**p**

Print the addressed line(s). Unless the **-n** command
line option is used, this command will cause duplica-
tion of the line in the output. Also, used when commands change flow control (*d*, N, b).

[*address1*][,*address2*]**P**

Print first part (up to embedded newline) of multi-line
pattern created by **N** command. Same as **p** if **N** has
not been applied to a line.

---

q

[*address*]**q**

Quit when *address* is encountered. The addressed line is first written to output, along with any text appended to it by previous **a** or **r** commands.

---

r

[*address*]**r** *file*

Read contents of *file* and append after the contents of the pattern space. Exactly one space must separate the **r** and the filename.

---

s

[*address1*][,*address2*]**s**/*pattern*/*replacement*/[*flags*]

Substitute *replacement* for *pattern* on each addressed line. If pattern addresses are used, the pattern // represents the last pattern address specified. The following flags can be specified:

g   replace all instances of /*pattern*/ on each addressed line, not just the first instance.

p   print the line if a successful substitution is done. If several successful substitutions are done, multiple copies of the line will be printed.

w *file*   write the line to a *file* if a replacement was done. A maximum of 10 different *files* can be opened.

---

t

[*address1*][,*address2*]**t** [*label*]

Test if successful substitutions have been made on addressed lines, and if so, branch to *label*. (See **b** and **:**.) If label is not specified, drop to bottom of list of editing commands.

---

w

[*address1*][,*address2*]**w** *file*

Write contents of pattern space to *file*. This action occurs when the command is encountered rather than

---

when the pattern space is output. Exactly one space must separate the **w** and the filename. A maximum of 10 different files can be opened.	**w** *continued*
*[address1][,address2]***x** Exchange contents of the pattern space with the contents of the hold space.	**x**
*[address1][,address2]***y**/*abc*/*xyz*/ Transform each character by position in string *abc* to its equivalent in string *xyz*.	**y**

Editors

awk

awk [*options*] [program] [parameters] [files]

awk is a pattern-matching *"program"* for modifying files. It takes the following options on the command line:
   -f*file*   use patterns contained in *file*.
   -F*c*   use field separator

awk also accepts parameters such as x= ... y= ... on the input line.

An *awk* program consists of patterns and procedures:

   pattern {*procedure*}

Both are optional. If *pattern* is missing, {*procedure*} will be applied to all lines. If {*procedure*} is missing, the line will be passed unaffected to standard output (i.e., it will be printed as is).

Each input line, or *record*, is divided into *fields* by white space (blanks or tabs) or by some other user-definable record separator. Fields are referred to by the variables **$1, $2, ... , $***n*. **$0** refers to the entire record.

Shell variables can be passed as parameters inside an *awk* program.

   FILE = *$File*

passes the value of the shell variable *File* into an *awk* variable named *FILE*.

Patterns

Patterns can be specified using regular expressions as described in Section 3.

   pattern {*procedure*}

- The special pattern **BEGIN** allows you to specify procedures that will take place *before* the first input line is processed. (Generally, you set global variables here.)

- The special pattern **END** allows you to specify procedures that will take place *after* the last input record is read.

- ^ and $ can be used to refer to the beginning and end of a field, respectively, rather than the beginning and end of a line.

- A pattern can evaluate expressions using any of the relationals operators <, <=, ==, !=, >=, and > or pattern matching operators ~ and ~!. For example: **$2 > $1** selects lines for which the second field is greater than the first. Comparisons can be either string or numeric.

- Patterns can be combined with the Boolean operators || (or), && (and), and ! (not).

- Patterns can include any of the predefined special variables listed below. For example: **NF > 1** selects records with more than one field.

Special Variables

FS	field separator (blanks and tabs by default)
RS	record separator (newline by default)
OFS	output field separator (blanks by default)
ORS	output record separator (newline by default)
NR	number of current record
NF	number of fields in current record
$0	entire input record
$1, $2, ..., $n	first, second, ... nth field in current record, where fields are separated by **FS**.

Editors

Procedures

Procedures consist of one or more commands, functions, or variable assignments, separated by newlines or semicolons, and contained within curly braces. Commands fall into four groups:

- variable or array assignments

- printing commands

- built-in functions

- control-flow commands

Variables and Array Assignments

Variables can be assigned a value with an = sign. For example:

FS = ","

Expressions using the operators +, -, /, and % (modulo) can be assigned to variables.

Arrays can be created with the **split** function (see below) or can be simply named in an assignment statement. **++, +=,** and **-=** are used to increment or decrement an array, as in the C language. Array elements can be subscripted with numbers (*array*[1], ... ,*array*[n]) or with names. For example, to count the number of occurrences of a pattern, you could use the following program:

/pattern/ {*n*["*/pattern/*"]++}
END {print *n*["*/pattern/*"] }

String constants such as *filenames* must be quoted. Shell variables can be referred to by placing the variables inside double quotes, then single quotes: **" '$LOGNAME' "**.

break Exit from a **while** or **for** loop.	**break**
continue Begin next iteration of **while** or **for** loop without reaching the bottom.	**continue**
exit Do not execute remaining instruction and read no new input. END procedures will be executed.	**exit**
$x = $ **exp**(arg) Return exponent of *arg*.	**exp**
for $(i=lower;i<=upper;i++)$ *command* While the value of variable i is in the range between *lower* and *upper*, do *command*. A series of commands must be put within braces. "$<=$" or any relational operator can be used; "$++$" or "$--$" can be used to decrement variable.	**for**
for (*item* **in** *array*) *command* For each *item* in an associative *array*, do *command*. More than one command must be put inside braces. Refer to each element of the array as *array[item]*.	**for**

Editors

if	**if** *(condition)*
	    command
	[**else**]
	    [*command*]
	
	If *condition* is true, do *command(s)*, otherwise do *command* in **else** clause. Condition can be an expression using any of the relational operators <, <=, ==, !=, >=, or >, as well as the pattern-matching operator ~ (e.g. "if $1 ~ /[Aa].*/"). A series of commands must be put within braces.

int	$x = \mathbf{int}(arg)$ Return integer value of *arg*.
length	$x = \mathbf{length}(arg)$ Return the length of *arg*. If *arg* is not supplied, $0 is assumed. Therefore, **length** can be used as a predefined variable that contains the length of the curren record.
log	$x = \mathbf{log}(arg)$ Return logarithm of *arg*.
next	**next** Read next input line and start new cycle through pattern/procedures statements.
print	**print** [*args*] Print *args* on output. *Args* is usually one or more fields, but may also be one or more of the predefined variables. Literal strings must be quoted. Fields are

printed in the order they are listed. If separated by commas in the argument list, they are separated in the output by the character specified by **OFS**. If separated by spaces, they are concatenated in the output.

print
continued

printf

printf

Formatted print statement. Fields or variables can be formatted according to instructions in the *format* argument. The number of arguments must correspond to the number specified in the format sections.

Format follows the conventions of the C-language *printf* statement. Here are a few of the most common formats:

%s	a string
%d	a decimal number
%*n***.m***f*	a floating point number; n = total number of digits. m = number of digits after decimal point.
%[-]*nc*	n specifies minimum field length for format type c, while - justifies value in field; otherwise value is right justified.

Format can also contain embedded escape sequences: **\n** (newline) or **\t** (tab) being the most common.

Spaces and literal text can be placed in the *format* argument by quoting the entire argument. If there are multiple expressions to be printed, there should be multiple formats specified. An example is worth a thousand words. For an input file containing only the line:

5 5

The program:

{printf ("The sum on line %s is %d \n", NR, $1+$2)}

will produce:

The sum on line 1 is 10.

followed by a newline.

Editors

split	x = **split**(*string,array*[*,sep*])
	Split string into elements of array **array[1],...,array[n]**. String is split at each oc-currence of separator *sep*. If *sep* is not specified, **FS** is used. The number of array elements created is re-turned.
sprintf	x = **sprintf**("*format*", *expression*)
	Return the value of *expression*(s), using the specified *format* (see **printf**).
sqrt	x = **sqrt**(*arg*)
	Return square root of *arg*.
substr	x = **substr**(*string,m,*[*n*])
	Return substring of *string* beginning at character po-sition *m* and consisting of the next *n* characters. If *n* is omitted, include all characters to the end of string.
while	**while** *(condition)* *command*
	Do *command* while *condition* is true (see **if** for a description of allowable conditions). A series of commands must be put within braces.

5

Nroff and Troff

This section is divided into four subsections, each covering a different facet of the *nroff/troff* formatting system. These sections are:

- *nroff/troff* requests.
- Escape sequences.
- Predefined number registers.
- Special characters.

See Section 1 for command line options for the various commands.

nroff and *troff* are UNIX's postprocessing programs for formatting text files. *nroff* is designed to format output for line and letter-quality printers, *troff* for typesetting. Except for some functions that are specific to typesetting, the same commands work for both programs.

In addition, we make references to *ditroff*, or *device-independent troff*, which is a later version of *troff*. For the most part, *ditroff* works the same as *troff*; where there are distinctions, the original *troff* is referred to as *otroff*.

Formatting is specified by embedding brief codes into the text source file. These codes act as directives to *nroff* and *troff* when they are invoked. A typical code, to center the following line of text, would be typed in as follows:

```
.ce
This text should be centered.
```

The output would appear as follows:

This text should be centered.

There are two types of formatting codes, referred to respectively as *primitives* and *macros*. The primitives (also called *requests*) allow direct control of almost any feature of page layout and formatting; however, they are sometimes difficult to use. The macros are predefined combinations of primitives designed to create a total effect.

See Section 6 for more information on macros.

.ab [*text*]   **.ab**

Abort and print *text* as message. If *text* is not
specified, the message "User Abort" is printed.

.ad [*c*]   **.ad**

Adjust one or both margins. *c* can be:
    b or **n** adjust both margins.
    c   center all lines.
    l   adjust left margin only.
    r   adjust right margin only.

Without argument, return to previous adjustment.
The current adjustment mode is stored in register **.j**,
with the following values: 0=l, 1=b, 3=c, 5=r. (See
.na).

.af *r c*   **.af**

Assign format *c* to register *r*. *c* can be:
    1   0, 1, 2, etc.
    001   000, 001, 002, etc.
    i   lowercase Roman.
    I   uppercase Roman.
    a   lowercase alphabetic.
    A   uppercase alphabetic.

.am *xx* [*yy*]   **.am**

Append to macro *xx*; end append at call of *yy*
{Default *yy*=..}.

.as	**.as** *xx string* Append *string* to string register *xx*. *string* may contain spaces, and is terminated by a newline. An initial quote (") is ignored.
.bd	**.bd** [s] *f n* Overstrike characters in font *f n* times, or if **s** is specified, characters in special font *n* times when font *f* is in effect.
.bp	**.bp** [*n*] Begin new page. Number next page *n*.
.br	**.br** Break to a new line (output partial line).
.c2	**.c2** *c* Set no-break control character to *c*. (Certain requests beginning with **.** cause a break; starting these requests with *c* will not cause a break.) {Default is '}.
.cc	**.cc** *c* Set control character that introduces requests and macros to *c*. {Default is .}.

.ce [*n*]

Center next *n* lines; if *n* is 0, stop centering. *n* applies only to lines containing output text. Blank lines do not count. {Default *n*=1}.

.cf *file*

Copy contents of file into output, uninterpreted (*ditroff* only).

.ch *xx* [*n*]

Change trap position for macro *xx* to *n*. If *n* is absent, remove the trap.

.cs *f n m*

Use constant spacing for font *f*. Constant character width will be *n*/36 ems. If *m* is given, the em is taken to be *m* points.

.cu [*n*]

Continuous underline (including inter-word spaces) on next *n* lines. If *n* is 0, stop underlining (italicize in *troff*). Use **.ul** to underline visible characters only. Underline font can be switched in *troff* with **.uf** request. However, you must use a macro to underline in *troff*.

.da [*xx*]

Divert following text, appending it to macro *xx*. If no argument, end diversion.

Nroff/Troff

.de	**.de** *xx* [*yy*]
	Define macro *xx*. End definition at *yy*. {Default *yy*=..}
.di	**.di** [*xx*]
	Divert following text to newly defined macro *xx*. If no argument, end diversion.
.ds	**.ds** *xx string*
	Define *xx* to contain *string*.
.dt	**.dt** *n xx*
	Install diversion trap at position *n* within diversion to invoke macro *xx*.
.ec	**.ec** [*c*]
	Set escape character to *c*. {Default \}
.el	**.el**
	Else portion of **if-else** (See **.ie** below).
.em	**.em** *xx*
	Set end macro to be *xx*. *xx* will automatically be executed when all other output has been completed.

.eo

Turn escape character mechanism off. All escape characters will be printed literally.

.eo

.ev [*n*]

Change environment to *n*. If no argument, restore previous environment. 0≤*n*≤2 {initial value 0}. You must return to the previous environment by using **.ev** with no argument, or you will get a stack overflow.

.ev

.ex

Exit from formatter and perform no further text processing. Typically used with **.nx** for form-letter generation.

.ex

.fc *a b*

Set field delimiter to *a* and pad character to *b*.

.fc

.fi

Turn on fill mode. {Default is on} (See **.nf**).

.fi

.fl

Flush output buffer. Used for interactive debugging.

.fl

.fp *n f*

Assign font *f* to position *n*. In *otroff*, *n* is from 1 to 4. In *ditroff*, it is from 1 to 9.

.fp

Nroff/Troff

.ft	**.ft** *f* Change font to *f*, where *f* is a one- or two-character font name, or a font position assigned with **.fp**.
.hc	**.hc** [*c*] Change hyphenation-indication character to *c*. {Default –}
.hw	**.hw** *words* Specify hyphenation points for *words*. (e.g. **.hw spe-ci-fy**).

.hy	**.hy** *n*
	
	Turn hyphenation on (*n*≥1) or off (*n*=0).
	    n=1 hyphenate whenever necessary
	    n=2 don't hyphenate last word on page
	    n=4 don't split off first two characters
	    n=8 don't split off last two characters
	    n=14 use all three restrictions
	(See **.nh**).

.ie	**.ie** [!]*condition anything* **.el** *anything* If portion of *if-else*. If *condition* is true, do *anything*. Otherwise do *anything* following **.el** request. **.ie/.el** pairs can be nested. Syntax for *condition* is as described below under **.if**.
.if	**.if** [!]*condition anything* If *condition* is true, do *anything*. The presence of an ! negates the condition. The following conditions can

be used:

.if
continued

o	true if the page number is odd
e	true if the page number is even
n	true if the processor is **nroff**
t	true if the processor is **troff**
"*str1*"*str2*"	true if *str1* is identical to *str2*. (Often used to test the value of arguments passed to a macro.)
expr	true if the value of expression *expr* is greater than zero

Expressions typically contain number register interpolations, and can use any of the following operators:

+,-,/,*	standard arithmetic operators
%	modulo
>,<	greater than, less than
>=,<=	greater than or equal, less than or equal
=,==	equal
&	logical AND
:	logical OR

If *anything* runs over more than one line, it can be delimited by \{ and \}. For example,

---

.ig [*yy*]

.ig

Ignore following text, up to line beginning with *yy*. Default *yy* is **..**, as with **.de**. Useful for commenting out large blocks of text or macro definition.

.in [±][*n*]

.in

Set indent to *n* or increment indent by ±*n*. If no argument, restore previous indent. Current indent is stored in register **.i**.

.it *n xx*

.it

Set input line count trap to invoke macro *xx* after *n* lines of input text have been read.

Nroff/Troff

.lc	**.lc** *c*
	Set leader repetition character to *c*.

.lg	**.lg** *n*
	Turn ligature mode on if *n* is absent or non-zero.

.ll	**.ll** [±][*n*]
	Set line length to *n* or increment line length by ±*n*. If no argument, restore previous line length. Current line length is stored in register **.l**.{Default 6.5 inches}

.ls	**.ls** [*n*]
	Set line spacing to *n*. If no argument, restore previous line spacing. {Initial value 1}

.lt	**.lt** [*n*]
	Set title length to *n*. If no argument, restore previous value.

.mc	**.mc** [*c*] [*n*]
	Set margin character to *c*, and place it *n* spaces to the right of margin. If *c* is missing, turn margin character off. If *n* is missing, use previous value. Initial value for *n* is .2 inches in *nroff* and 1 em in *troff*.

.mk	**.mk** [*r*]
	Mark current vertical place in register *r*. Return to mark with **.rt** or **.sp**\\ n*r*.

.na   .na

Do not adjust margins (See **.ad**). Current adjustment
mode is stored in register **.j**.

.ne *n*   .ne

If *n* lines do not remain on this page, start new page.

.nf   .nf

Do not fill or adjust output lines (See **.ad** and **.fi**).

.nh   .nh

Turn hyphenation off (See **.hy**).

.nm [*n m s i*]   .nm

Number output lines (*n*≥0) or turn it off (*n*=0). ±*n*
sets initial line number; *m* sets numbering interval; *s*
sets separation of numbers and text; *i* sets indent of
text. (See **.nn**).

.nn *n*   .nn

Do not number next *n* lines, but keep track of
numbering sequence, which can be resumed with
.nm+0. (See **.nm**).

.nr *r n* [*m*]   .nr

Assign the value *n* to number register *r* and optionally set auto increment to *m*.

Nroff/Troff

.ns	**.ns** Turn no-space mode on (See **.rs**).
.nx	**.nx** *file* Switch to *file* and do not return to current file (See **.so**).
.os	**.os** Output saved space specified in previous **.sv** request.
.pc	**.pc** *c* Set page number character to *c*.
.pi	**.pi** *cmd* Pipe output to *cmd* instead of placing it on standard output (*ditroff* and *nroff* only).
.pl	**.pl** [±][*n*] Set page length to *n* or increment page length by ±*n*. If no argument, restore default. Current page length is stored in register **.p**. {Default 11 inches}
.pm	**.pm** Print names and sizes of all defined macros.

.pn [±][*n*]

Set next page number to *n* or increment page number by ±*n*. Current page number is stored in register %.

.po [±][*n*]

Offset text a distance of *n* from left edge of page, or else increment the current offset by ±*n*. If no argument, return to previous offset. Current page offset is stored in register .o.

.ps *n*

Set point size to *n* (*troff* only). Current point size is stored in register .s. {Default 10 points}

Nroff/Troff

.rd [*prompt*]

Read input from terminal, after printing optional *prompt*.

.rm *xx*

Remove macro or string *xx*.

.rn *xx yy*

Rename request, macro, or string *xx* to *yy*.

.rr *r*

Remove register *r*.

.rs	**.rs** Restore spacing (turn no-space mode off — see **.ns**).
.rt	**.rt** [±*n*] Return (upward only) to marked vertical place, or to ±*n* from top of page or diversion (See **.mk**).
.so	**.so** *file* Switch out to *file*, then return to current file (See **.nx**).
.sp	**.sp** *n* Leave *n* blank lines. {Default is 1}
.ss	**.ss** *n* Set space-character size to *n*/36 em (no effect in *nroff*).
.sv	**.sv** *n* Save *n* lines of space; output saved space with **.os**.
.sy	**.sy** *cmd* [*args*] Execute UNIX command *cmd* with optional arguments (*ditroff* only).

.ta *n*[*t*] *m*[*t*] ...

Set tabstops at positions *n*, *m*, etc. If *t* is not given,
tab is left-adjusting; *t* can be:
   L   left adjust.
   R   right adjust.
   C   center.

.tc *c*

Define tab output character as *c* (e.g., **.tc** . will draw
a string of dots to tab position). {Default is white
space}

.ti [±][*n*]

Indent next output line *n* spaces, or increment the
current indent by ±*n* for the next output line.

.tl '*l*'*c*'*r*'

Specify left, centered, or right title. Title length is
specified by **.lt**, not **.ll**.

.tm *text*

Terminal message. (Print *text* on standard error.)

.tr *ab*

Translate character *a* to *b*.

Nroff/Troff

.uf	.uf *f*
	Set underline font to *f* (to be switched to by **.ul** or **.cu**). {Default is *italics*}
.ul	.ul [*n*]
	Underline (italicize in *troff*) next *n* input lines. Do not underline inter-word spaces. Use **.cu** for continuous underline. Underline font can be switched in *troff* with **.uf** request. However, you must use a macro to underline in *troff*.
.vs	.vs [*n*]
	Set vertical line spacing to *n*. If no argument, restore previous spacing. Current vertical spacing is stored in register **.v**. {Default 1/6 inch in *nroff*, 12 points in *troff*}
.wh	.wh *n* [*xx*]
	When position *n* is reached, execute macro *xx*; negative values are with respect to page bottom. If *xx* is not supplied, remove any trap(s) at that location. (Two traps can be at the same location if one is moved over the other with **.ch**. They cannot be placed at the same location with **.wh**.)

Sequence	Effect
\\	To prevent or delay the interpretation of \
\e	Printable version of the current \ escape character
\'	´ (acute accent); equivalent to \(aa
\`	` (grave accent); equivalent to \(ga
\-	– Minus sign in the current font
\.	Period (dot)
\(space)	Unpaddable space-size space character
\(newline)	Concealed (ignored) newline
\0	Digit width space
\\|	1/6-em narrow space character (zero width in *nroff*)
\^	1/12-em half-narrow space character (zero width in *nroff*)
\&	Non-printing, zero width character
\!	Transparent line indicator
\"	Beginning of comment
\$*n*	Interpolate argument 1≤*n*≤9
\%	Default optional hyphenation character
\(*xx*	Character named *xx*
*x, *(*xx*	Interpolate string *x* or *xx*
\a	Non-interpreted leader character
\b´*abc*...´	Bracket building function
\c	Make next line continuous with current
\d	Forward (down) 1/2-em vertical motion (1/2 line in *nroff*)
\D´l *x,y*´	Draw a line from current position to coordinates *x,y*. (*ditroff* only)
\D´c *d*´	Draw circle of diameter *d* with left edge at current position. (*ditroff* only)
\D´e *d1 d2*´	Draw ellipse with horizontal diameter *d1* and vertical diameter *d2*, with left edge at current position. (*ditroff* only)
\D´a *x1 y1 x2 y2*´	Draw arc counterclockwise from current position, with center at *x1,y1* and endpoint at *x1+x2,y1+y2*. (*ditroff* only)
\D´~ *x1 y1 x2 y2* ...´	Draw spline from current position through the specified coordinates. (*ditroff* only)
\f*x*,\f(*xx*,\f*n*	Change to font named *x* or *xx* or to position *n*
\h´*n*´	Local horizontal motion; move right *n* or if *n* is negative move left

Nroff/Troff

Sequence	Effect
\H´n´	Set character height to *n* points, without changing width. (*ditroff* only)
\kx	Mark horizontal *input* place in register *x*
\l´nc´	Draw horizontal line of length *n* (optionally with *c*)
\L´nc´	Draw vertical line of length *n* (optionally with *c*)
\nx,\n(xx	Interpolate number register *x* or *xx*
\o´abc...´	Overstrike characters *a*, *b*, *c*...
\p	Break and spread output line
\r	Reverse 1-em vertical motion (reverse line in *nroff*)
\sn,\s±n	Change point-size to *n* or increment by *n*. \s0 returns to previous point size.
\S´n´	Slant output *n* degrees to the right. Negative values slant to the left. A value of zero turns off slanting. (*ditroff* only)
\t	Non-interpreted horizontal tab
\u	Reverse (up) 1/2-em vertical motion (1/2 line in *nroff*)
\v´n´	Local vertical motion; move down *n* or if *n* is negative move up
\w´string´	Interpolate width of *string*
\x´n´	Extra line-space function (*n* negative provides space before, *n* positive provides after)
\zc	Print *c* with zero width (without spacing)
\{	Begin multi-line conditional input
\}	End multi-line conditional input
\x	*x*, any character *not* listed above

Predefined Number Registers

Read-Only Registers

.$	Number of arguments available at the current macro level
.$$	Process id of *troff* process (*ditroff* only)
.A	Set to 1 in *troff*, if **-a** option used; always 1 in *nroff*
.H	Available horizontal resolution in basic units
.T	Set to 1 in *nroff*, if **-T** option used; always 0 in *troff*; in *ditroff*, the string *(.T contains the value of **-T**.
.V	Available vertical resolution in basic units
.a	Post-line extra line-space most recently utilized using \x´N´
.c	Number of *lines* read from current input file
.d	Current vertical place in current diversion; equal to **nl**, if no diversion
.f	Current font as physical quadrant (1 to 4 in *otroff*; 1 to 9 in *ditroff*)
.h	Text base-line high-water mark on current page or diversion
.i	Current indent
.j	Current adjustment mode
.l	Current line length
.n	Length of text portion on previous output line
.o	Current page offset
.p	Current page length
.s	Current point size
.t	Distance to the next trap
.u	Equal to 1 in fill mode and 0 in no-fill mode
.v	Current vertical line spacing
.w	Width of previous character
.x	Reserved version-dependent register
.y	Reserved version-dependent register
.z	Name of current diversion

Nroff/Troff

Read-Write Registers

%	Current page number
ct	Character type (set by *width* function)
dl	Width (maximum) of last completed diversion
dn	Height (vertical size) of last completed diversion
dw	Current day of the week (1 to 7)
dy	Current day of the month (1 to 31)
hp	Current horizontal place on *input* line
ln	Output line number
mo	Current month (1 to 12)
nl	Vertical position of last printed text base line
sb	Depth of string below base line (generated by *width* function)
st	Height of string above base line (generated by *width* function)
yr	Last two digits of current year

On the Standard Fonts

Char	Input	Character Name
,	´	close quote
'	`	open quote
—	\(em	3/4 Em dash
-	–	hyphen or
-	\(hy	hyphen
–	\-	current font minus
•	\(bu	bullet
□	\(sq	square
_	\(ru	rule
¼	\(14	1/4
½	\(12	1/2
¾	\(34	3/4
fi	\(fi	fi ligature
fl	\(fl	fl ligature
ff	\(ff	ff ligature
ffi	\(Fi	ffi ligature
ffl	\(Fl	ffl ligature
°	\(de	degree
†	\(dg	dagger
´	\(fm	foot mark
¢	\(ct	cent sign
®	\(rg	registered
©	\(co	copyright

Nroff/Troff

The Special Font

Char	Input	Character Name
§	\(sc	section
´	\(aa	acute accent
`	\(ga	grave accent
_	\(ul	underrule
→	\(->	right arrow
←	\(<-	left arrow
↑	\(ua	up arrow
↓	\(da	down arrow
|	\(br	box rule
‡	\(dd	double dagger
☞	\(rh	right hand
☜	\(lh	left hand
○	\(ci	circle
⊕	\(vs	visible space indicator (*ditroff* only)

Bracket Building Symbols

Char	Input	Character Name
⌠	\(lt	left top of big curly bracket
⎨	\(lk	left center of big curly bracket
⌡	\(lb	left bottom of big curly bracket
⌐	\(rt	right top of big curly bracket
⎬	\(rk	right center of big curly bracket
⌐	\(rb	right bottom of big curly bracket
⌈	\(lc	left ceiling (left top) of big square bracket
|	\(bv	bold vertical
⌊	\(lf	left floor left bottom of big square bracket
⌉	\(rc	right ceiling (right top) of big square bracket
⌋	\(rf	right floor (right bottom) of big square bracket

Char	Input	Character Name
+	\(pl	math plus
−	\(mi	math minus
=	\(eq	math equals
*	\(**	math star
/	\(sl	slash (matching backslash)
√	\(sr	square root
	\(rn	root en extender
≥	\(>=	greater than or equal to
≤	\(<=	less than or equal to
≡	\(==	identically equal
≈	\(~~	approx equal
~	\(ap	approximates
≠	\(!=	not equal
×	\(mu	multiply
÷	\(di	divide
±	\(+-	plus-minus
∪	\(cu	cup (union)
∩	\(ca	cap (intersection)
⊂	\(sb	subset of
⊃	\(sp	superset of
⊆	\(ib	improper subset
⊇	\(ip	improper superset
∞	\(if	infinity
∂	\(pd	partial derivative
∇	\(gr	gradient
¬	\(no	not
∫	\(is	integral sign
∝	\(pt	proportional to
∅	\(es	empty set
∈	\(mo	member of
|	\(or	or

Greek Characters

Char	Input	Char Name	Char	Input	Char Name
α	\(*a	alpha	A	\(*A	ALPHA
β	\(*b	beta	B	\(*B	BETA
γ	\(*g	gamma	Γ	\(*G	GAMMA
δ	\(*d	delta	Δ	\(*D	DELTA
ε	\(*e	epsilon	E	\(*E	EPSILON
ζ	\(*z	zeta	Z	\(*Z	ZETA
η	\(*y	eta	H	\(*Y	ETA
θ	\(*h	theta	Θ	\(*H	THETA
ι	\(*i	iota	I	\(*I	IOTA
κ	\(*k	kappa	K	\(*K	KAPPA
λ	\(*l	lambda	Λ	\(*L	LAMBDA
μ	\(*m	mu	M	\(*M	MU
ν	\(*n	nu	N	\(*N	NU
ξ	\(*c	xi	Ξ	\(*C	XI
o	\(*o	omicron	O	\(*O	OMICRON
π	\(*p	pi	Π	\(*P	PI
ρ	\(*r	rho	P	\(*R	RHO
σ	\(*s	sigma	Σ	\(*S	SIGMA
ς	\(ts	terminal sigma			
τ	\(*t	tau	T	\(*T	TAU
υ	\(*u	upsilon	Y	\(*U	UPSILON
φ	\(*f	phi	Φ	\(*F	PHI
χ	\(*x	chi	X	\(*X	CHI
ψ	\(*q	psi	Ψ	\(*Q	PSI
ω	\(*w	omega	Ω	\(*W	OMEGA

The Special Font

6

Macro Packages

This section is divided into three subsections, each covering a different macro package of the *nroff/troff* formatting system. These sections are:

- The *-mm* macro package.
- The *-ms* macro package.
- The *-me* macro package.

Macros are predefined combinations of primitives designed to create a total effect. For example, a macro might specify the format for a heading by defining (in *troff*) the font size and style, the amount of space above and below, and some form of automatic section numbering.

Macro packages are organized, internally consistent groups of macros. There are three widely-available macro packages: *-mm*, *-ms*, and *-me*. They are named by the *nroff/troff* options that invoke them.

Only *-mm* is officially supported as a part of System V. The version of *-ms* that is documented here is the extended version of *-ms* shipped with Berkeley UNIX systems, not the the original Bell Labs *-ms* macros, which are no longer officially supported by AT&T.

See Section 5 for more information on *nroff/troff* primitives, escape sequences, special characters, and number registers.

-mm Macros

.1C	**.1C** Return to single-column format.
.2C	**.2C** Start two-column format.
.AE	**.AE** End abstract. (See .AS).
.AF	**.AF** [*company name*] Alternate format for first page. Change first-page "Subject/Date/From" format. If argument is given, other headings are not affected. No argument suppresses company name and headings.
.AL	**.AL** [*type*] [*indent*] [**1**] Initialize numbered or alphabetized list. Specify *list*, *type*, and *indent* of text. If 3rd argument is 1, spacing between items is suppressed. Mark each item in list with **.LI**; end list with **.LE**. *type*

Within the .AL entry:

type

1	arabic numbers
A	upper-case letters
a	lower-case letters
I	roman numerals, upper-case
i	roman numerals, lower-case

Default is numbered listing. Default text indent is specified in register **Li**.

.AS *[type][n]*

Start abstract of specified *type*, indenting *n* spaces. (Used with **.TM** and **.RP** only.) End with **.AE**.

type

1   abstract on cover sheet and first page
2   abstract only on cover sheet
3   abstract only on Memorandum for File cover sheet.

.AS

.AT *title*

Author's *title* appears after author's name in formal memoranda.

.AT

.AU *name*

Author's *name* and other information (up to nine arguments) supplied at beginning of formal memoranda.

.AU

.AV *name*

Approval signature line for *name*. Closing macro in formal memoranda.

.AV

.B *[barg]* *[parg]* . . .

Set *barg* in bold (underline in *nroff*) and *parg* in previous font; up to 6 arguments.

.B

.BE

End bottom block and print after footnotes (if any), but before footer. (See **.BS**).

.BE

.BI	**.BI** [*barg*] [*iarg*] Set *barg* in bold (underline in *nroff*) and *iarg* in italics; up to 6 arguments.
.BL	**.BL** [*indent*] [**1**] Initialize bullet list. Specify indent of text. Default indent specified in register *Pi* (3). If 2nd argument is 1, suppress blank line between items.
.BR	**.BR** [*barg*] [*rarg*] Set *barg* in bold (underline in *nroff*) and *rarg* in Roman; up to 6 arguments.
.BS	**.BS** Begin block of text to be printed at bottom of page, after footnotes (if any), but before footer. End with **.BE**.
.CS	**.CS** [*pgs*] [*other*] [*tot*] [*figs*] [*tbls*] Cover sheet information supplied for formal memoranda.
.DE	**.DE** End static or floating display started with **.DS** or **.DF**.
.DF	**.DF** [*type*] [*mode*] [*rindent*] Start floating display. (Default format type is no indent and no-fill mode.) *rindent* is amount line

length is decreased to bring text in from right margin.
End with **.DE.**

type

> **L or 0**
>> no indent
> **I or 1** indent standard amount
> **C or 2**
>> center each line individually
> **CB or 3**
>> center as a block

mode

> **N or 0**
>> no-fill mode
> **F or 0**
>> fill mode

If the amount of space required to output text is
greater than the space remaining on page, the display
will be saved for the next page while text following
the display will be used to fill the current page. See
also **De** and **Df** registers.

.DL [*indent*] [**1**]

Initialize dashed list. Specify indent of text. Default
indent specified in register *Pi* (3). If 2nd argument is
1, suppress blank line between items.

.DS [*type*] [*mode*] [*rindent*]

Start static display. (Default format type is no indent
and no-fill mode.) *rindent* is amount line length is
decreased to bring text in from right margin. End
with **.DE.** See **.DF** for possible values for *type* and
mode.

If the amount of space required to output text is
greater than the space remaining on the current page,
then a page break will cause the display to start at the
top of the next page. See also **.DF.**

.EC	**.EC** [*caption*] [*n*] [*flag*]
	Equation *caption*. Arguments optionally override default numbering, where *flag* determines use of number *n*. (See **.EQ**).
	flag
	0 *n* is a prefix to number {Default}
	1 *n* is a suffix
	2 *n* replaces number
.EF	**.EF** ['*left*'*center*'*right*']
	Print three-part string as even page footer; parts are left-justified, centered and right-justified at bottom of every even page.
.EH	**.EH** ['*left*'*center*'*right*']
	Print three-part string as even page header; parts are left-justified, centered and right-justified at top of every even page.
.EN	**.EN**
	End equation display. (See **.EQ**).
.EQ	**.EQ** [*text*]
	Start equation display to be processed by *eqn* using *text* as label. (See **.EC**). End with **.EN**. See Section 7 for more information on *eqn*.
.EX	**.EX** [*caption*] [*n*] [*flag*]
	Exhibit *caption*. Arguments optionally override default numbering, where *flag* determines use of

number *n*.	**.EX**
flag	*continued*
0 *n* is a prefix to number {Default}	
1 *n* is a suffix	
2 *n* replaces number	

.FC [*text*]	**.FC**
Use *text* for formal closing.	

.FD [*0-11*]	**.FD**
Set default footnote format.	

.FE	**.FE**
End footnote. (See **.FS**).	

.FG [*title*]	**.FG**
Figure *title* follows.	

.FS [*c*]	**.FS**
Start footnote using *c* for indicator. {Default is numbered footnote} End with **.FE**.	

.H *n* [*heading*]	**.H**
Numbered *heading* level *n*, where *n* is from 1 to 7. See number registers **Ej** (page eject), **Hb** (break after heading), **Hc** (centered heading), **Hi** (type of first paragraph after heading), **Hs** (space after heading), **Hu** (unnumbered headings), the strings **HF** (font	

Macros

☞

Macro Packages

.H *continued*	control) and **HP** (point size) and the macro **.HM** (heading mark). See also **.HU** (unnumbered headings), **.HX**, **.HY** and **.HZ** (user-supplied macros invoked during output of header).
.HC	**.HC** [*c*] Use *c* as hyphenation indicator.
.HM	**.HM** [*mark*] Heading *mark* style follows Arabic (**1** or **001**), Roman (**i** or **I**), or Alpha (**a** or **A**).
.HU	**.HU** *heading* Unnumbered *heading* follows. Same as **.H** except that no heading mark is printed. See register **Hu**.
.HX	**.HX** User-supplied exit macro executed before printing heading.
.HY	**.HY** User-supplied exit macro executed in middle of printing heading.
.HZ	**.HZ** User-supplied macro executed after heading.

.I [*iarg*] [*parg*]   **.I**

Set *iarg* in italics (underline in *nroff*) and *parg* in previous font. Up to 6 arguments.

.IA   **.IA**

Start inside (recipient's) address for business letter. End with **.IE**.

.IB [*iarg*] [*barg*]   **.IB**

Set *iarg* in italics (underline in *nroff*) and *barg* in bold. Up to 6 arguments.

.IE   **.IE**

End inside (recipient's) address for business letter (See **.IA**).

Macros

.IR [*iarg*] [*rarg*]   **.IR**

Set *iarg* in italics (underline in *nroff*) and *rarg* in Roman. Up to 6 arguments.

.LB *n m pad type* [*mark*]   **.LB**

List beginning. Allows complete control over list format. Begin each item in list with **.LI**; end the list with **.LE**.

    n   text indent
    m   mark indent
    pad padding associated with mark

.LB
continued

type

if 0, use the specified *mark*. If non-zero, and *mark* is 1, A, a, I, i, list will be automatically numbered or alphabetically sequenced. In this case, *type* controls how the *mark* will be displayed. For example, if *mark* is currently 1, *type* will have the following results:

Type	Result
1	1.
2	1)
3	(1)
4	[1]
5	<1>
6	{1}

mark

the symbol or text that will be used to start each list entry. *mark* can be null (creates hanging indent), a text string, or 1, A, a, I or i to create an automatically numbered or lettered list (see .AL).

LI-space

the number of blank lines to be output between each following .LI macro. {Default 1}

LB-space

the number of blank lines to be output by the LB macro itself. {Default 0}

.LC

.LC [*n*]

Clear list level up to *n*.

.LE

.LE [1]

End item list. (See .AL, .BL, .LB, .ML, and .VL). An argument of 1 produces a line of white space (.5v) after the list.

.LI [*mark*] [1]
text

Item in list. List must be initialized (see **.AL**, **.BL**,
.LB, **.ML**, and **.VL**) and then closed using **.LE**. If
mark is specified then it replaces mark set by list-
initialization macro. If mark is specified along with
2nd argument of 1, then mark is prefixed to current
mark.

.LI

.LO *type* [*notation*]

Specify *type* and string to appear as *notation* in business letter.

type

AT	attention
CN	confidential
RN	reference
SA	salutation
SJ	subject

.LO

.LT [*type*]

Business letter type.

type

BL	blocked (default)
SB	semi-blocked
FB	full-blocked
SP	simplified

.LT

Macros

.ML *mark* [*indent*] [1]

Initialize list with specified *mark*, which may be one
or more characters. Specify indent of text; default is
one space wider than mark. If 3rd argument is 1,
omit space between items in list.

.ML

.MT	**.MT** [*type*] [*title*]
	
	Specify memorandum *type* and *title*. Controls format of formal memoranda and must be specified after other elements, such as **.TL, .AF, .AU, .AS,** and **.AE.** User-supplied *title* is prefixed to page number.
	
	type
	
	    0 no type
	    1 Memorandum for file {Default}
	    2 Programmer's notes
	    3 Engineer's notes
	    4 Released paper
	    5 External letter
	    string *string* is printed

.ND	**.ND** *date* New Date. Change date that appears in formal memoranda.
.NE	**.NE** Notation end. (See .NS)
.nP	**.nP** Numbered paragraphs with double-line indent at start of paragraph. See also .P.
.NS	**.NS** [*type*] Notation start. Used with **.MT 1** and **.AS 2/.AE** (memorandum for file) to specify note for cover sheet. Otherwise used at end of formal memoranda. Specify notation *type*.

0	Copy to {Default}
1	Copy (with attention) to
2	Copy (without att.) to
3	Att.
4	Atts.
5	Enc.
6	Encs.
7	Under Separate Cover
8	Letter to
9	Memorandum to
10	Copy (with atts.) to
11	Copy (without atts.) to
12	Abstract Only to
13	Complete Memorandum to

string copy *string* to

.OF ['*left*' *center*' *right*']   **.OF**

Print three-part string as odd page footer; parts are left-justified, centered and right-justified at bottom of every odd page.

.OH ['*left*' *center*' *right*']   **.OH**

Print three-part string as odd page header; parts are left-justified, centered and right-justified at bottom of every odd page.

.OK [*topic*]   **.OK**

Other keywords. Specify *topic* to appear on cover sheet of formal memoranda. Up to 9 arguments.

.OP   **.OP**

Force an odd page.

.P	**.P** [*type*]
	
	Start new paragraph. A paragraph *type* can be specified, overriding default.
	
	type
	
	    0 left-justified {Default}
	    1 indented
	    2 indented except after displays, lists, and headings (**.H, .LC, .DE**).
	
	Default paragraph type for document is set through register **Pt**; its default value is 0. The amount of indent is set through register **Pi**; its default is 3. The amount of spacing between paragraphs is set through the register **Ps**, which is one line of white space. For numbered paragraphs, set the register **Np** to 1.

.PF	**.PF** ['*left*'*center*'*right*'] Print three-part string as footer; parts are left-justified, centered and right-justified at bottom of every page. Use \\\\nP in string to obtain page number. See also **.EF** and **.OF**.
.PH	**.PH** ['*left*'*center*'*right*'] Print three-part string as header; parts are left-justified, centered and right-justified at top of every page. Use \\\nP in string to obtain page number. See also **.EH** and **.OH**.

.PM	**.PM** [*type*]
	
	Proprietary marking on each page.
	
	type
	
	    P private
	    N notice

.PX

Page-heading user exit. Invoked after restoration of default environment. See **.TP**.

.R

Return to Roman font (end underlining in *nroff*).

.RB [*rarg*] [*barg*]

Set *rarg* in Roman and *barg* in bold. Up to 6 arguments.

.RD [*prompt*]

Read input from terminal, supplying optional *prompt*.

.RF

End of reference text. (See **.RS**).

.RI [*rarg*] [*barg*]

Set *rarg* in Roman and *barg* in italics. Up to 6 arguments.

.RL [*indent*] [**1**]

Initialize reference list, essentially a numbered list with number set within brackets ([ ]). Specify indent of text; default is set through register **Li** (6). If 2nd argument is 1, omit space between list items.

Macros

.RP	.RP
	Produce reference page.
.RS	.RS [*n*]
	Start automatically numbered reference, with optional specified reference number *n*. End with **.RF**.
.S	.S [±] [*n*] [±] [*m*]
	Set point size to *n* and vertical spacing to *m* (*troff* only). Alternatively, either argument can be specified by incrementing or decrementing current value (**C**), default value (**D**), or previous value (**P**). {Defaults: point size = 10, vertical spacing = 12}
.SA	.SA [*n*]
	Set right margin justification to *n*. {Defaults: no justification for *nroff*, justification for *troff*}
	n
	0 no justification
	1 justification.
.SG	.SG [*name*]
	Use name for signature line.
.SK	.SK *n*
	Skip *n* pages.

.SM *x* [*y z*]

Reduce string *x* by one point. If strings *y* and *z* are also specified, *y* is reduced by one point.

.SP [*n*]

Output *n* blank vertical spaces. The spacing requests of two consecutive **.SP** macros do not accumulate.

.TB [*title*][*n*][*flag*]

Supply table *title*. Arguments optionally override default numbering, where *flag* determines use of number *n*.

flag

0	*n* is a prefix to number {Default}
1	*n* is a suffix
2	*n* replaces number

.TC [*slevel*] [*spacing*] [*tlevel*] [*tab*] [*head1*] . . .

Generates table of contents in format specified by arguments. The levels of headings that are saved for table of contents is determined by setting the Cl register.

slevel and *spacing* determine levels of headings that have spacing before them and the amount of spacing. Default is 1; first-level headings have a blank line before them.

tlevel and *tab* affect location of page number. Heading levels less than or equal to *tlevel* are output with page numbers at right margin; otherwise heading and page number are separated by two spaces. If page numbers are at right margin, and if *tab* is 0, a leader will be output using dots; otherwise, spaces are used.

Macros

.TE	**.TE** End table. (See .TS).
.TH	**.TH [N]** Table header ends. Must be used with .TS H. **N** suppress table headers until new page.
.TL	**.TL** *title* Supply title for formal memoranda.
.TM	**.TM** [*n*] Supply number *n* for formal memoranda.
.TP	**.TP** Page top macro, invoked automatically at the beginning of a new page. Executed in environment in which heading is output. See .PH.
.TS	**.TS [H]** Start table to be processed by *tbl*. End with .TE. See Section 7 for more information on *tbl*. **H** put table header on all pages. End entry of table header with .TH.
.TX	**.TX** User-supplied macro executed before table-of-contents titles.

.TY

User-supplied macro executed before table-of-contents header.

.VL *n* [*m*] [1]

Initialize variable item list. Used to produce indented or labeled paragraphs. Indent text *n* spaces and indent mark *m* spaces. If 3rd argument is 1, omit space between list items. Begin each item with **.LI**, specifying *mark* for each item; end list with **.LE**.

.VM [*n*] [*m*]

Add *n* lines to top margin and *m* lines to bottom.

.WA

Start of writer's address in business letter. End with **.WE**.

.WE

End of writer's address in business letter (See **.WA**).

.WC [*x*]

Change column or footnote width to *x*.

x

FF	all footnotes same as first
-FF	turn off FF mode
N	normal default mode
WD	wide displays

Macros

.WC *continued*	**-WD** use default column mode
	WF wide footnotes
	-WF turn off WF mode

Predefined String Names

BU	Bullet; same as \(bu.
Ci	List of indents for table of contents levels.
DT	Current date, unless overridden. Month, day, year (e.g., July 28, 1986).
EM	Em dash string (em dash in *troff* and a double hyphen in *nroff*).
F	Footnote number generator.
HF	Fonts used for each level of heading. [1=Roman, 2=Italic, 3=Bold]
HP	Point size used for each level of heading.
Le	Title set for "List Of Equations".
Lf	Title set for "List Of Figures".
Lt	Title set for "List Of Tables".
Lx	Title set for "List Of Exhibits".
RE	SCCS Release and Level of *-mm*.
Rf	Reference number generator.
Rp	Title for References.
TM	Trademark string. Places the letters "TM" one-half line above the text that it follows.

\

A dagger (†) next to a register name indicates that the register can *only* be set from the command line or before the *-mm* macro definitions are read by the formatter. Any register that has a single-character name can be set from the command line with the **-r** option.

A†	If set to 1, omits technical memorandum headings and provides spaces appropriate for letterhead. See **.AF** macro.
Au	Inhibits author information on first page. See **.AU** macro.
C†	Flag indicating type of copy (original, draft, etc.).
Cl	Level of headings saved for table of contents. See **.TC** macro. {Default 2}
Cp	If set to 1, list of figures and tables appear on same page as table of contents. Otherwise, they start on a new page. {Default 1}
D†	If set to 1, sets debug mode. {Default 0} If set, *-mm* will continue even when it encounters normally fatal errors.
De	If set to 1, ejects page after each floating display. {Default 0}
Df	Format of floating displays. See **.DF** macro.
Ds	Sets the pre- and post-space used for static displays.
E†	Font for the Subject/Date/From: 0=Bold; 1=Roman. {Default 0}
Ec	Equation counter, incremented for each **.EC** macro.
Ej	Heading level for page eject before headings. {Default=0, no eject}
Eq	If set to 1, places equation label at left margin. {Default 0}
Ex	Exhibit counter, incremented for each **.EX** macro.
Fg	Figure counter, incremented for each **.FG** macro.
Fs	Vertical spacing between footnotes.
H1-H7	Heading counters for levels 1-7, incremented by the **.H** macro of corresponding level or the **.HU** macro if at level given by the **Hu** register. The **H2-H7** registers are reset to 0 by any **.H** (or **.HU**) macro at a lower-numbered level.
Hb	Level of heading for which break occurs before output of body text. {Default 2 lines}
Hc	Level of heading for which centering occurs. {Default 0}
Hi	Indent type after heading. Legal values are: 0 left-justified, 1 indented, 2 indented except after **.H**, **.LC**, **.DE**. {Default 1}
Hs	Level of heading for which space after heading occurs. {Default 2}
Ht	Numbering type of heading: single (1) or concatenated (0). {Default 0}
Hu	Sets level of heading at which unnumbered headings occur. {Default 2}
Hy	Sets hyphenation. If set to 1, enables hyphenation. {Default 0}
L†	Sets length of page. {Default 66v}
Le	Flag for list of equations following table of contents. 0 = do not print; 1 = print. {Default 0}

Macros

Lf	Flag for list of figures following table of contents. 0 = do not print; 1 = print. {Default 0}
Li	Default indent of lists. {Default 5}
Ls	List spacing between items by level. {Default 6 = spacing between all levels of list}
Lt	Flag for list of tables following table of contents. 0 = do not print; 1 = print {Default 0}
Lx	Flag for list of exhibits following table of contents. 0 = do not print; 1 = print {Default 0}
N†	Page numbering style. 0=all pages get header; 1=header printed as footer on page 1; 2=no header on page 1; 3=section-page as footer; 4=no header unless .PH has been invoked; 5=section-page and section-figure as footer. {Default 0}
Np	Numbering style for paragraphs. 0 = unnumbered; 1 = numbered.
O	Offset of page. For *nroff*, this value is an unscaled number representing character positions. {Default 9 (7.5i)} For *troff*, this value is scaled. {Default .5i}
Oc	Table of contents page numbering style. 0=lowercase Roman; 1=Arabic. {Default 0}
Of	Figure caption style. 0=period separator; 1=hyphen separator. {Default 0}
P	Current page number.
Pi	Amount of indent for paragraph. {Default 5 for *nroff*, 3 for *troff*}
Ps	Amount of spacing between paragraphs. {Default 3v}
Pt	Paragraph type. Legal values are: 0 left-justified, 1 indented, 2 indented except after .H, .LC, .DE. {Default 0}
Pv	Inhibits "PRIVATE" header.
Rf	Reference counter, incremented for each .RS.
S†	Default point size for *troff*. {Default 10} (Vertical spacing is \nS+2)}
Si	Standard indent for displays. {Default 5 for *nroff*, 3 for *troff*}
T†	Type of *nroff* output device. Causes register settings for specific devices.
Tb	Table counter, incremented for each .TB.
U†	Underlying style (*nroff*) for .H and .HU. If not set, use continuous underline, otherwise, don't underline punctuation and white space. {Default 0}
W†	Width of page (line and title length). {Default 6i}

─── Other Reserved Macro and String Names ───

In *-mm*, the only macro and string names you can safely use are names consisting of a single lowercase letter, or two character names whose first character is a lowercase letter and whose second character is *anything but* a lowercase letter. Of these, only **c2** and **nP** are already used.

-mm Macros

This section documents the extended version of -*ms* shipped with Berkeley UNIX systems, not the the original Bell Labs -*ms* macros, which are no longer officially supported by AT&T.

.1C

Return to single-column format. This macro necessarily causes a page break as well. (See .2C and .MC).

.2C

Start two-column format. Return to single-column with .1C.

.AB

Begin abstract in cover sheet. End abstract with .AE.

.AE

End abstract begun with .AB.

.AI *name*

Print name of author's institution. Generally follows .AU in a cover sheet sequence; may be repeated up to nine times for multiple author/institution pairs.

.AU *name*

Print author's name. Generally follows .TL and precedes .AI in a cover sheet sequence; may be repeated

---

Macros

.AU *continued*	up to nine times for multiple authors.
.B	**.B** [*text*] Print *text* in boldface. If *text* is missing, equivalent to **.ft 3**.
.B1	**.B1** Enclose following text in a box. End box with **.B2**.
.B2	**.B2** End boxed text. (See **.B1**).
.BD	**.BD** Start block display. Display text is printed exactly as it appears in the source file, centered around the longest line. (Same as **.DS B**.) End with **.DE**.
.BR	**.BR** Start bibliographic format (used to precede bibliographic record).
.BX	**.BX** *word* Surround *word* in a box. It generally does not work for more than one word at a time, due to problems with filling. To box more than one word, separate them with an unpaddable space (\ ).

.CD

Start centered display. Each line in the display is individually centered. (Same as **.DS C.**) End with **.DE.**

.DA

Print today's date as the center footer of each page.

.DE

End displayed text.

.DS [*type*]

Start displayed text. End with **.DE.**

type

    B   left-justified block, centered (See **.BD**).
    C   centered display (See **.CD**).
    I   indented display (See **.ID**). {Default}
    L   left-centered display (See **.LD**).

Macros

.EQ

Begin equation to be processed by *eqn*. End with **.EN.** See Section 7 for more information on *eqn*.

.EN

End equation. (See **.EQ**).

.FS	**.FS** Start footnote. Text of footnote follows on succeeding lines. End with **.FE**.
.FE	**.FE** End footnote. (See **.FS**).
.GO	**.GO** Start processing text. This macro performs various package startup procedures. Cover sheet macros should precede **.GO** to appear on a separate page.
.I	**.I** [*text*] Print *text* in italics. If *text* is missing, equivalent to **.ft 2**.
.ID	**.ID** Start indented display. Text is printed exactly as it is in the source file, but indented 8 ens. (Same as **.DS I**). End with **.DE**.
.IP	**.IP** *label n* Indent paragraph *n* spaces with hanging *label*. **.RS** and **.RE** can be used for nested indents.
.KE	**.KE** End of keep or floating keep. (See **.KF** and **.KS**).

.KF

Begin floating keep. End with **.KE**. Enclosed text will stay on the same page, and if it will not fit on the current page, succeeding text will "float" above it in the output.

.KF

.KS

Start keep. End with **.KE**. Enclosed text will stay on the same page. If text will not fit on the current page, a page break will occur.

.KS

.LD

Start left-justified display. Block is centered, but individual lines are left justified in the block. (Same as **.DS L.**) End with **.DE.**

.LD

.LG

Increase type size by two points (*troff* only). Restore normal type with **.NL.**

.LG

.LP

Start block paragraph. Interparagraph spacing determined by register **PD** {Default .5v in *troff*, 1 line in *nroff*}

.LP

.MC *cw gw*

Start multi-column mode, with column-width *cw* and gutter width *gw*. As many columns will be generated as will fit in the current line length. Return to single-column mode with **.1C.**

.MC

.ND	**.ND** Suppress printing of date. (See .DA)
.NH	**.NH** *n* *heading text* Numbered section heading; level *n* of the section number is automatically incremented.
.NL	**.NL** Restore default type size (*troff* only). Used after .LG or .SM.
.PP	**.PP** Start standard indented paragraph. Size of paragraph indent is stored in register **PI** {Default 5 ens}.
.QE	**.QE** End quoted paragraph. See .QP and .QS.
.QP	**.QP** Quoted paragraph: indented on both sides, with blank lines above and below, and (in *troff*) with the type size reduced by 1 point.
.QS	**.QS** Quoted paragraph, retaining current point size and vertical spacing. End with .QE.

.R [*text*]

Print *text* in Roman. If *text* is missing, equivalent to
.ft R.

.R

.RE

End one level of relative indent. (See **.RS**).

.RE

.RP

Initiate title page for a "released paper."

.RP

.RS

Right Shift. Increase relative indent one level. End
with **.RE**. Often used with **.IP**.

.RS

.SB *word chars*

Subscript *word* with *chars*. (See **.SU**).

.SB

Macros

.SG

Print a signature line.

.SG

.SH
heading text

Unnumbered section heading.

.SH

.SM	**.SM** Change to smaller type size (*troff* only). Restore normal type with **.NL**.
.SU	**.SU** *word chars* Superscript *word* with *chars*. (See **.SB**).
.TE	**.TE** End table to be processed by *tbl*. (See **.TS**).
.TH	**.TH** End of table header. Must be used with **.TS H**.
.TL	**.TL** *multiple line title* Title line(s) for cover sheet. A multi-line title can be specified; it is terminated by the next macro (usually **.AU** in the cover sheet sequence.
.TS	**.TS [H]** Start table to be processed by *tbl*. End table with **.TE**. See Section 7 for more information on *tbl*. **H** put table header on all pages. End entry of table header with **.TH**.
.UL	**.UL** Underline following text, even in *troff*.

Number Registers for Page Layout

BI	Bibliographical indent. {Default 3 ens}
CW	Column width. {Default 7/15 of line length}
FL	Footnote length. {Default 11/12 of line length}
FM	Bottom margin. {Default 1 inch}
GW	Intercolumn gap. {Default 1/15 of line length}
HM	Top margin. {Default 1 inch}
LL	Line length. {Default 6 inches}
LT	Title length. {Default 6 inches}
PD	Paragraph spacing. {Default 0.3 of vertical spacing}
PI	Paragraph indent. {Default 5 ens}
PO	Page offset. {Default 26/27 inches}
PS	Point size. {Default 10 point}
QI	Quotation indent. {Default 5 ens}
VS	Vertical line spacing. {Default 12 point}

Reserved Macro and String Names

The following macro and string names are used by the **ms** package. Avoid using these names for compatibility with the existing macros. An italicized *n* means that the name contains a numeral (generally the interpolated value of a number register).

,	.]	:	[.	[c	[o	^	'	~
1C	2C	AB	AE	AI	A*n*	AT	AU	AX
B	B1	B2	BB	BG	BT	BX	C	C1
C2	CA	CC	CF	CH	CM	CT	DA	DW
DY	EE	EG	EL	EM	EN	E*n*	EQ	EZ
FA	FE	FF	FG	FJ	FK	FL	FN	FO
FS	FV	FX	FY	HO	I	IE	IH	IM
I*n*	IP	IZ	KD	KF	KJ	KS	LB	LG
LP	LT	MC	ME	MF	MH	MN	MO	MR
ND	NH	NL	NP	OD	OK	PP	PT	PY
QE	QF	QP	QS	R	R3	RA	RC	RE
R*n*	RP	RS	RT	S0	S2	S3	SG	SH
SM	SN	SY	TA	TC	TD	TE	TH	TL
TM	TQ	TR	TS	TT	TX	UL	US	UX
WB	WH	WT	XF	XK	XP			

Reserved Number Register Names

The following number register names are used by the **ms** package. An italicized *n* means that the name contains a numeral (generally the interpolated value of another number register).

*n*T	AJ	AV	BC	BD	BE	BH	BI	BQ
BW	CW	EF	FC	FL	FM	FP	GA	GW
H1	H2	H3	H4	H5	HM	HT	I0	IF
IK	IM	IP	IR	IS	IT	IX	I*n*	J*n*
KG	KI	KM	L1	LE	LL	LT	MC	MF
MG	ML	MM	MN	NA	NC	ND	NQ	NS
NX	OJ	PD	PE	PF	PI	PN	PO	PQ
PS	PX	QI	QP	RO	SJ	ST	T.	TB
TC	TD	TK	TN	TQ	TV	TY	TZ	VS
WF	XX	YE	YY	ZN				

Note that with the exception of [c and [o, none of the number register, macro, or string names contain lowercase letters, so lower or mixed case names are a safe bet when you're writing your own macros.

.1c

Return to single-column format. (See **.2c**.)

.2c

Enter two-column format. Force a new column with **.bc**; end two-column mode with **.1c**.

.ar

Set page number in Arabic.

.b *w x*

Set *w* in bold and *x* in previous font (underline in *nroff*).

.(b *type*

Begin block keep. End with **.)b**.

type

C	centered block keep
F	filled block keep
L	left-justified block keep

.)b

End block keep. (See **.(b**).

.ba	**.ba** *n* Set the base indent to *n*.
.bc	**.bc** Begin column (used after **.2c**).
.bi	**.bi** *w x* Set *w* in bold italics and *x* in previous font.
.bl	**.bl** *n* Leave *n* contiguous white space. Equivalent to **.sp** *n* inside a block.
.bx	**.bx** *w x* Set *w* in a box and *x* immediately outside the box.
.+c	**.+c** *title* Begin chapter with *title*.
.$c	**.$c** *title* Begin numbered chapter with *title*.
.$C	**.$C** *keyword n title* User-definable macro. Called by **.$c**, supplying *keyword* (e.g., "Chapter" or "Appendix"); chapter or

appendix number (*n*), and *title*.	.$C *continued*

.(c   .(c

Begin centered block. End with **.)c**.

.)c   .)c

End centered block.

.(d   .(d

Begin delayed text. End with **.)d**.

.)d   .)d

End delayed text. Print text with **.pd**.

.ef '*l*'*c*'*r*'   .ef

Print three-part footer on all *even* pages. Parts are
left-justified, centered and right-justified at bottom of
every even page.

.eh '*l*'*c*'*r*'   .eh

Print three-part heading on all *even* pages. Parts are
left-justified, centered and right-justified at top of
every even page.

.ep   .ep

End this page and print footnotes.

Macros

.EN	**.EN** End equation. (See **.EQ**).

.EQ	**.EQ** *type title*
	
	Begin equation to be processed by *eqn* of specified *type*, and with specified *title* printed on the right margin next to the equation. End with **.EN**. See Section 7 for more information on *eqn*.
	
	type
	
	    C centered.
	    I indented.
	    L left justified.

.$f	**.$f** Call to print footer.
.(f	**.(f** Begin text for footnote. End with .)f.
.)f	**.)f** End of footnote text.
.fo	**.fo** '*l*'*c*'*r*' Print three-part footer on *all* pages. Parts are left-justified, centered and right-justified at bottom of every page.

.$H   .$H

Normally undefined macro, called immediately before
printing text on a page. Can be used for column
headings, etc.

.$h   .$h

Call to print header.

.he '*l*'*c*'*r*'   .he

Print three-part heading on *all* pages. Parts are left-
justified, centered and right-justified at top of every
page.

.hl   .hl

Draw a horizontal line length of page.

.hx   .hx

Do not print headings and footers on next page.

.i *w x*   .i

Set *w* in italics and *x* in previous font (underline in
nroff).

.ip *label n*   .ip

Indent paragraph *n* spaces with hanging label.

Macro Packages

.ix	.ix [±*n*] Indent, no break. Equivalent to 'in *n*.

.(l	.(l *type*
	
	Begin list. End with .)l.
	type
	    C centered list
	    F filled list
	    L left-justified list

.)l	.)l End list. (See .(l).
.ll	.ll +*n* Set line length to +*n* (all environments).
.lo	.lo Loads another set of macros which is intended to be a set of locally defined macros.
.lp	.lp Begin block paragraph (left-justified).
.m1	.m1 *n* Set *n* spaces between top of page and heading.

.m2 *n*

.m2

Set *n* spaces between heading and first line of text.

.m3 *n*

.m3

Set *n* spaces between footer and text.

.m4 *n*

.m4

Set *n* spaces between footer and bottom of page.

.n1

.n1

Number lines in margin beginning with 1.

.n2*n*

.n2*n*

Number lines in margin beginning with *n*; stop numbering if *n* is 0.

.np

.np

Numbered paragraphs.

.of '*l*'*c*'*r*'

.of

Print three-part footer on *all* odd pages. Parts are left-justified, centered and right-justified at bottom of every odd page.

Macros

.oh	**.oh** '*l*'*c*'*r*' Print three-part heading on *all* odd pages. Parts are left-justified, centered and right-justified at top of every odd page.
.$p	**.$p** *title n d* Print section heading with specified *title*, section number *n*, and depth of section *d*.
.$0	**.$0** *title n d* Called automatically after every call to **.$p**. Normally undefined, but may be used to automatically put every section title into table of contents, or for some similar function.
.$1-.$6	**.$1-.$6** Traps called just before printing that depth section. These macros are called from **.$p**.
.pa	**.pa** [±*n*] Equivalent to **.bp**.
.pd	**.pd** Print delayed text (indicated by **.(d** and **.)d**).
.pp	**.pp** Begin indented paragraph.

.q *w x*	**.q**
Surround *w* with double quotes and *x* immediately outside quotes.	
.(q	**.(q**
Begin major quote. End with .)q.	
.)q	**.)q**
End major quote.	
.r *w x*	**.r**
Set *w* in Roman font and *x* in previous font.	
.rb *w x*	**.rb**
Set *w* in bold and *x* in previous font.	
.re	**.re**
Reset tabs to every 0.5 inches in *troff* and every 0.8 inch in *nroff*.	
.ro	**.ro**
Set page number in Roman numerals.	
.$s	**.$s**
Separate footnotes with 1.5-inch horizontal line.	

Macros

.sh	**.sh** Begin numbered section heading.
.sk	**.sk** Leave next page blank.
.sx	**.sx** +*n* Begin a paragraph at level *n*.
.sz	**.sz** *n* Set character point size to *n* (line spacing set proportionally).
.th	**.th** Initialize for a thesis.
.tp	**.tp** Initialize for a title page.
.TS	**.TS [H]** Start table. End with **.TE**. See Section 7 for more information on *tbl*. **H** put table header on all pages. End entry of table header with **.TH**.

.TH

Table header ends. Must be used with **.TS H**.

.TH

.TE

End table. (See **.TS**).

.TE

.u *w x*

Underline *w* and set *x* in previous font.

.u

.uh *title*

Begin unnumbered section heading using *title*.

.uh

.(x

Begin index entry.

.(x

.)x

End index entry. Print with **.xp**.

.)x

.)x_

No page number for index.

.)x_

.x1 *n*

Set the line length to *n* (current environment only).

.x1

Macros

.xp	**.xp** Print index. (See **.(x)**.
.(z	**.(z** Begin floating keep.
.)z	**.)z** End floating keep.
.++	**.++** *type header* Defines the section of the paper being entered.

7

Preprocessors

This section is divided into three subsections, each covering a different preprocessor of the *nroff/troff* formatting system. These sections are:

- The *tbl* preprocessor.
- The *eqn* preprocessor.
- The *pic* graphics language.

See Section 1 for command line options for the various commands.

Each of these preprocessors translate code into *nroff/troff* requests and escape sequences; run independently of the formatter, they can be used to confirm that syntax is correct, or to determine where it fails. For example, to run *tbl* alone on the command line, use the command,

    tbl *file*

tbl

The success of a table to be processed by *tbl* depends largely on the header lines, which consist of one line listing the options and one or more format lines. Each field of the table input must be separated by a tab or designated tab symbol, with each row input entirely on a single line unless a field is enclosed by "T{" and "T}".

tbl Macros

.TS	Start table.
.TE	End table.
.TS H	Used when the table will continue onto more than one page. Used with .TH to define a header that will print on every page.
.TH	With .TS H, ends the header portion of the table.
.T&	Continue table after changing format line.

Options

Options affect the entire table. The options should be separated by commas, and the option line must be terminated by a semicolon.

center	Center with *current* margins.
expand	Flush with current right *and* left margins.
(*blank*)	Flush with current left margin (Default).
box	Enclose table in a box.
doublebox	Enclose table in two boxes.
allbox	Enclose each table entry in a box.
tab (*x*)	Define the tab symbol as *x*.
linesize *n*	Set lines or rules (e.g., from box) to *n* point type.
delim *xy*	Recognize *x* and *y* as the *eqn* delimiters.

The format line affects the layout of individual columns and rows of the table. Each line contains a key letter for each column of the table. The column entries should be separated by spaces, and the format section must be terminated by a period. Each line of format corresponds to one line of the table, except for the last, which corresponds to all following lines up to the next .T&, if any.

Key letters:

c   Center.

l   Left justify.

r   Right justify.

n   Align numerical entries.

a   Align alphabetic subcolumns.

s   Horizontally span previous column entry across this column.

^   Vertically continue entry from previous row down through this row.

Other options (must follow a key letter):

b   Boldface.

i   Italics.

fx Font x.

pn Point size.

t   Begin any corresponding vertically spanned table entry at the top line of its range.

e   Equal width columns.

w(n)   Minimum column width. Also used with text blocks. n can be given in any acceptable *troff* units.

vn Vertical line spacing. Used *only* with text blocks.

n   Amount of separation between columns {Default is 3n}.

| Single vertical line. Typed between key letters.

‖   Double vertical line. Typed between key letters.

_   Single horizontal line. Used in place of a key letter.

=   Double horizontal line. Used in place of a key letter.

Preprocessors

The data portion includes both the heading and text of the table. Each table entry must be separated by a tab symbol.

xx	*troff* requests may be used (such as **.sp** #, **.ce** #, etc.).
\	As last character in a line, combine following line with current line (hide newline).
\^	Vertically spanned table entry. Span table entry immediately above down over this row.
_ or =	As the only character in a line, extend a single or double horizontal line the full width of the table.
\$_ or \$=	Extend a single or double horizontal line the full width of the column.
_	Extend a single horizontal line the width of the *contents* of the column.
\R*x*	Print *x*'s as wide as the *contents* of the column.
... [*tab*]T{	Start text block as a table entry. Must end a line. Necessary when a line of text is input over more than one line, or will span more than one line of output.
... T}[*tab*]	End text block. Must begin a line.

A tbl Example

Input:

```
.TS
center,box,linesize (6),tab(@);
cb s s.
Horizontal Local Motions
_
.T&
ci | ci s
ci | ci s
ci | ci | ci
c | l s.
Function@Effect in
\^@_
\^@troff@nroff
_
\eh'n'@Move distance N
\e(space)@Unpaddable space-size space
\e0@Digit-size space
_
.T&
c | l | l.
\e|@1/6 em space@ignored
\e^@1/12 em space@ignored
.TE
```

Result:

Horizontal Local Motions		
Function	*Effect in*	
	troff	*nroff*
\h'n'	Move distance N	
\(space)	Unpaddable space-size space	
\0	Digit-size space	
|	1/6 em space	ignored
\^	1/12 em space	ignored

eqn

eqn is a preprocessor designed to facilitate the typesetting of mathematical equations.

.EQ   Start Typesetting Mathematics.

.EN   End Typesetting Mathematics.

Character Translations

The character sequences below are recognized and translated as shown.

Char	Trans	Char	Trans
>=	$\geq$	approx	$\approx$
<=	$\leq$	nothing	
==	$\equiv$	cdot	$\cdot$
!=	$\neq$	times	$\times$
+-	$\pm$	del	∇
->	$\rightarrow$	grad	∇
<-	$\leftarrow$	...	$\ldots$
<<	$\ll$	,...,	$,\ldots,$
>>	$\gg$	sum	$\sum$
inf	∞	int	$\int$
partial	∂	prod	$\prod$
half	$^1/_2$	union	$\cup$
prime	$'$	inter	$\cap$

Digits, parenthesis, brackets, punctuation marks, and the following words are converted to Roman font when encountered:

    sin cos tan sinh cosh tanh
    arc max min lin log ln
    exp Re Im and if for det

Greek letters can be printed in upper or lower case. To obtain Greek letters, simply spell them out:

Char	Trans	Char	Trans
alpha	α	tau	τ
beta	β	upsilon	υ
gamma	γ	phi	φ
delta	δ	chi	χ
epsilon	ε	psi	ψ
zeta	ζ	omega	ω
eta	η	GAMMA	Γ
theta	θ	DELTA	Δ
iota	ι	THETA	Θ
kappa	κ	LAMBDA	Λ
lambda	λ	XI	Ξ
mu	μ	PI	Π
nu	ν	SIGMA	Σ
xi	ξ	UPSILON	Y
omicron	o	PHI	Φ
pi	π	PSI	Ψ
rho	ρ	OMEGA	Ω
sigma	σ		

The following words translate to marks on the tops of characters.

Char	Trans
x dot	$\dot{x}$
x dotdot	$\ddot{x}$
x hat	$\hat{x}$
x tilde	$\tilde{x}$
x vec	$\vec{x}$
x dyad	$\overleftrightarrow{x}$
x bar	$\bar{x}$
x under	$\underline{x}$

──Words Recognized by eqn──

above   Separate the pieces of a pile or matrix column.

back *n*   Move backwards horizontally *n* 1/100's of an 'm'.

bold   Change to bold font.

ccol   Center align a column of a matrix.

col???	Used with a preceding r or l to left or right adjust the columns of the matrix.
cpile	Make a centered pile (same as pile).
define	Create a name for a frequently used string.
delim	Define two characters to mark the left and right ends of an **EQN** equation to be printed in line.
down *n*	Move down *n* 1/100's of an 'm'.
fat	Widen the current font by overstriking it.
font *x*	Change to font *x* where *x* is the one character name or the number of a font.
from	Used in Summations, Integrals and similar constructions to signify the lower limit.
fwd *n*	Move forwards horizontally *n* 1/100's of an 'm'.
gfont *x*	Set a global font *x* for all equations.
gsize *n*	Set a global size for all equations.
up *n*	Move up *n* 1/100's of an 'm'.
italic	Change to italic font.
lcol	Left justify a column of a matrix.
left	Create big brackets, big braces, big bars, etc.
lineup	Line up marks in equations on different lines.
lpile	Left justify the elements of a pile.
mark	Remember the horizontal position in an equation. Used with lineup.
matrix	Create a matrix.
ndefine	Create a definition which only takes effect when **NEQN** is running.
over	Make a fraction.
pile	Make a vertical pile with elements centered above one another.
rcol	Right adjust a column of a matrix.
right	Create big brackets, big braces, big bars, etc.
roman	Change to Roman font.
rpile	Right justify the elements of a pile.
size *n*	Change the size of the font to *n*.
sqrt	Draw a square root sign.
sub	Start a subscript.
sup	Start a superscript.
tdefine	Make a definition which will apply only for **EQN**.

to	Used in Summations, Integrals and similar constructions to signify the upper limit.
~	Force extra space into the output.
^	Force a space one half the size of the space forced by ~ .
{ }	Force **EQN** to treat an element as a unit.
'...'	A string within quotes is not subject to alterations by **EQN**.

Precedence

If you don't use braces, **EQN** will do operations in the order shown in this list, reading from left to right.

dyad	*vec*	*under*	*bar*
tilde	*hat*	*dot*	*dotdot*
fwd	*back*	*down*	*up*
fat	*roman*	*italic*	*bold*
size	*sub*	*sup*	*sqrt*
over	*from*	*to*	

These operations group to the left:

over   sqrt   left   right

All others group to the right.

An eqn Example

Input:

```
.EQ
delim %%
.EN
%sum from i=0 to inf c sup i~=~lim from {m -> inf}
sum from i=0 to m c sup i%
```

Result:

$$\sum_{i=0}^{\infty} c^i = \lim_{m \to \infty} \sum_{i=0}^{m} c^i$$

pic

In **pic** there are often dozens of ways to draw a picture, not only because of the many permissible abbreviations, but because it tries to combine the language of geometry with English. You can specify a line, for example, with direction, magnitude, and starting point, yet often achieve the same effect by simply stating, "from *there* to *there*."

Full descriptions of primitive objects in **pic** can be ended by starting another line, or by the semi-colon character ("";""). A single primitive description can be continued on the next line, however, by ending the first with a backslash character (""\""). Comments may be placed on lines beginning with ""#"".

pic Macros

.PS [*h* [*w*]]	Start **pic** description. *h* and *w*, if specified, are the desired height and width of the picture; the full picture will be made to expand or contract to fill this space.
.PS <*file*	Read contents of *file* in place of current line.
.PE	End **pic** description.
.PF	End **pic** description and return to vertical position before matching **PS**.
.xx	*troff* request (or macro) *xx*.

Declarations

At the beginning of a **pic** description, you may declare a new scale, and declare any number of variables.

pic assumes you want a 1-to-1 scale, with 1 = one inch. You can declare a different scale, say 1 = one-*n*th of an inch, by declaring,
> **scale** = *n*

pic takes variable substitutions for numbers used in the description. Instead of specifying, ""**line right** *n*"", you may use a lower-case character as a variable, for example ""a"", by declaring at the top of the description:
> **a** = *n*

You may then write ""**line right a**"".

Primitives

Primitives may be followed by relevant options. Options are discussed later in this section.

arc [**cw**] [*options*] ["*text*"]
> A fraction of a circle {Default = 1/4 of a circle}. The **cw** option specifies a clockwise arc; default is counter-clockwise.

arrow [*options*] ["*text*"] [*then* ...]
> Draw an arrow. Essentially the same as **line ->**.

box [*options*] ["*text*"]
> Draw a box.

circle [*options*] ["*text*"]
> Draw a circle.

ellipse [*options*] ["*text*"]
> Draw an ellipse.

line [*options*] ["*text*"] [*then* ...]
> Draw a line.

move [*options*] ["*text*"]
> A move of position in the drawing. (Essentially, an invisible line).

spline [*options*] ["*text*"] [then ...]
> A line, with the feature that a "then" results in a gradual (sloped) change in direction.

"*text*"
> Text centered at current point.

Options

right [*n*] **left** [*n*] **up** [*n*] **down** [*n*]	Specifies direction of primitive; default is direction in which the previous description had been heading. Diagonals result by using two directions on the option line. Each direction can be followed by a specified length *n*.
rad *n* **diam** *n*	Specifies a primitive to have radius *n* (or diameter *n*).
ht *n* **wid** *n*	Specifies the height or width of the primitive to be *n*. For an arrow, line, or spline, refers to size of arrowhead.
same	Specifies a primitive of the same dimensions of the most recent matching primitive.

at *point*　　　　　　Specifies primitive to be centered at *point*.

with *.position* **at** *point*

Specifies the designated *position* of the primitive to be at *point*.

from *point1* **to** *point2*

Specifies the primitive to be drawn from *point1* to *point2*.

Points may be expressed as Cartesian coordinates or in respect to previous objects.

-> 　　　　　　　　　Specify the arrowhead to be directed forwards.

<- 　　　　　　　　　Specify the arrowhead to be directed backwards.

<-> 　　　　　　　　Specify the arrowhead to be directed both ways.

chop *n m*　　　　　Chop off *n* from beginning of primitive, and *m* from end. With only one argument, the same value will be chopped from both ends.

dotted　　　　　　　Specifies the primitive to be drawn dotted, dashed, or to be
dashed　　　　　　　invisible. Default is solid line.
invis

then . . .　　　　　　Continue primitive in a new direction. Relevant only to lines, splines, moves, and arrows.

──Text──────────────────────────

Text is be placed within quotes. To break the line, break into two (or more) sets of quotes.

Text always appears centered within the object, unless given one of the following arguments:

　　　　ljust　　　　　Text appears left-justified to the center.
　　　　rjust　　　　　Text appears right-justified to the center.
　　　　above　　　　Text appears above the center.
　　　　below　　　　Text appears below the center.

Object Blocks

A complex object which is the combination of several primitives (for example, an octagon) can be treated as a single object by declaring it as a block:

> **Object:** [
> description
>
> .
> .
> .
>
>]

Brackets are used as delimiters. Note that the object is declared as a proper noun, hence should begin with a capital letter.

Macros

The same sequence of commands can be repeated by using macros. The syntax is:

> **define** *sequence* %
> description
>
> .
> .
> .
>
> %

Here we have used the percent sign ("%") as the delimiter, but any character which is not in the description may be used.

Macros can take variables, expressed in the definition as "$1" through "$9". Invoke the macro with the syntax:

> *sequence(value1,value2, . . .)*

Positioning

In a **pic** description, the first action will begin at (0,0), unless otherwise specified with coordinates. Thus, the point (0,0) will move down and right on the drawing, as objects are placed above and left of the first object.

All points are ultimately translated by the formatter into x- and y-coordinates. You may therefore refer to a specific point in the picture by incrementing or decrementing by coordinates, i.e., "**2nd ellipse - (3,1)**".

You may refer to the x- and y-coordinates of an object by placing "**.x**" or "**.y**" at the end, for example, "**last box.x**" will refer to the x-coordinate of the most recent box drawn. Some of the physical attributes of the object may also be referred to similarly, as follows:

.x	x-coordinate of object's center
.y	y-coordinate of object's center
.ht	height of object
.wid	width of object
.rad	radius of object

Unless otherwise positioned, each object will begin at the point where the last object left off. If a command (or sequence of commands) is set off by curly braces ("{", "}"), however, **pic** will then return to the point before the first brace.

Positioning Between Objects

When referring to a previous object, you must use proper names. This can be done two ways:

1. By referring to it by order, e.g., **1st box, 3rd box, last box, 2nd last box**, etc.

2. By declaring it with a name, in initial caps, on its declaration line, e.g.,

     Line1: line 1.5 right from last box.sw

To refer to a point between two objects, or between two points on the same object, you may write:

  fraction **of the way between** *first.position* **and** *second.position*

or (abbreviated):

  fraction<first.position,second.position>

Corners

When you refer to a previous object, **pic** will assume that you mean the *center* of the object, unless you use a *corner* to specify a particular point on the object. The syntax used is:

  .corner **of** *object*

(for example, "**.sw of last box**"), or (abbreviated):

  object.corner

(for example, "**last box.sw**").

These corners may be:

n	north (same as "top")
s	south (same as "bottom")
e	east (same as "right")
w	west (same as "left")
ne	northeast
nw	northwest
se	southeast
sw	southwest
t	top (same as "north")
b	bottom (same as "south")
r	right (same as "east")
l	left (same as "west")
start	point where drawing of object began
end	point where drawing of object ended

You may also refer to the **upper right, upper left, lower right,** and **lower left** of an object.

——Numerical Operators———————————————

Several operators are functional in **pic**. These are:

+	addition
−	subtraction
*	multiplication
/	divided by
%	modulo

——Default Values———————————————

arcrad	0.25	**ellipsewid**	0.75
arrowwid	0.05	**linewid**	0.5
arrowht	0.1	**lineht**	0.5
boxwid	0.75	**movewid**	0.5
boxht	0.5	**moveht**	0.5
circlerad	0.25	**scale**	1
dashwid	0.05	**textht**	0
ellipseht	0.5	**textwid**	0

Input:

```
.PS
define smile %
a = $1
circle radius a at 0,0
arc cw radius a*.75 from a*.5,-a*.25 to -a*.5,-a*.25
"\(bu" at a*.33,a*.25
"\(bu" at a*-.33,a*.25
%
smile(.5)
.PE
```

Result:

pic

8

Program Debugging

This section covers the debugging programs provided for the UNIX environment: **adb** (absolute **debugger**) and **sdb** (symbolic **debugger**). These programs take an executable object file and its corefile, the core image file produced when *objfile* is executed. **adb** and **sdb** then provide a controlled environment for the execution of the program.

If *objfile* and *corefile* are not specified, **adb** and **sdb** take **a.out** as the default object file and **core** as the default core image file.

The adb Debugging Program

adb [-w] [*objfile*] [*corefile*]

-w   Create both *objfile* and *corefile* if necessary, making them read-write for **adb**.

Requests to **adb** are read from the standard input, of the general form:

[*address*] [, *count*] [*command*] [;]

The *dot* variable is set to *address* if it is specified; its default value is 0. *count* specifies how many times the command will be executed.

address and *count* are expressions of one of the forms described below.

Expressions

Expression	Value
.	The value of *dot*.
+	The value of *dot*, plus the current increment.
-	The value of *dot*, minus the current increment.
,,	The most recent *address*.
int	A decimal number, unless it begins with:
	0 Octal number.
	# Hexadecimal number.
int.frac	A 32-bit floating point number.
'*cccc*'	ASCII value of up to 4 characters.
<*x*	The value of *x*.
symbol	A sequence of characters, not starting with a digit.
(*exp*)	The value of *exp*.

Monadic Operators:

@	Contents of address in *objfile*.
*	Contents of address in *corefile*.
−	Integer negation.
~	Bitwise complement.

Dyadic Operators:

+	Addition.
-	Subtraction.
*	Multiplication.
%	Integer division.
&	Bitwise and.
|	Bitwise or.
#	Round up to next multiple.

Addresses

Addresses are interpreted according to the context in which they are used. A mapping from a written address to the file determines the file address. If the triples $(b1,e1,f1)$ and $(b2,e2,f2)$ represent the mapping for that file, the written address is calculated by the formula:

$$b1 \leq address < e1 = > file\ address = address + f1 - b1$$

or,

$$b2 \leq address < e2 = > file\ address = address + f2 - b2$$

Commands

Formatted Printing:

Command	Function
?format	Print from *objfile* according to *format*.
/format	Print from *corefile* according to *format*.
=format	Print the value of *dot* (current address).
[/?]l *expr mask*	Locate *expr* from *objfile* or *corefile* words masked with *mask*.
[/?]w *expr*	Write *expr* into *objfile* or *corefile*.

Debugging

Breakpoint and Program Control:

Command	Function
:b*c*	Set breakpoint at *dot* and execute command *c*.
:c*s*	Continue running program with signal *s*.
:d	Delete breakpoint.
:k	Kill the program being debugged.
:r	Run *objfile* under **adb** control.
:s*s*	Single step with signal *s*.

Miscellaneous Commands:

Command	Function
[?/]m *bl el fl*[?/]	Record new values for (*bl, el, fl*).
!*cmd*	Execute the command *cmd*.
>*name*	Assign *dot* to variable or register *name*.
$b	Print current breakpoints.
$c	C stack trace.
$d	Reset integer input to the default.
$e	External variables.
$<*f*	Read commands from file *f*.
$>*f*	Send output to file *f*.
$m	Print the address map.
$o	Treat input integers as octal.
$q	Exit from **adb**.
$r	General registers.
$s	Set offset for symbol match.
$v	Print **adb** variables in octal.
$w	Set output line width.

The adb Debugging Program

Format Summary

If no format is given in a command, the most recent format is used. *Format* consists of one or more characters specifying a style of printing. A decimal integer may precede each character, as a repeat count for the character. The *dot* variable is incremented by the amount given for each format character.

Character	Significance
a	The value of dot.
b	One byte in octal.
c	One byte as a character.
C	One byte as a character with 000 to 040 printed as @.
d	One word in decimal.
D	Long in decimal.
f	Two words in floating point.
F	Double in floating point.
i	Assembly instructions.
o	One word in octal.
O	Two words in octal.
q	Signed octal.
Q	Long signed octal.
p	The addressed value in symbolic form.
n	A newline.
r	A blank space.
s	A null terminated character string.
S	A string using the @ escape convention.
*n*t	Move to next *n* space tab.
u	One word as unsigned integer.
U	Long unsigned integer.
x	2 bytes in hexadecimal.
X	4 bytes in hexadecimal.
Y	Date.
^	Backup *dot*.
" ... "	Print the enclosed string.

Variables

Named variables are set initially by **adb** but are not used. Numbered variables are used as follows:

Variable	Value
0	The last value printed.
1	The last offset part of an instruction source.
2	The previous value of variable 1.

The system header in *corefile* sets the following variables on entry to **adb**:

Variable	Value
b	The base address of the data segment.
d	The data segment size.
e	The entry point.
m	The "magic" number.
s	The stack segment size.
t	The text segment size.

The sdb Debugging Program

sdb [**-w**] [**-W**] [*objfile* [*corefile* [*dir*]]]
    -w   overwrite locations in **objfile**.
    -W   do not warn if source files older than *objfile* cannot be found.

a "-" in place of *corefile* will force **sdb** to ignore any core image file.

sdb can be used to debug programs written in the C and F77 languages.

Commands

Formatted Printing:

t	Print a stack trace.
T	Print the top line of the stack trace.
variable/clm	Print variable according to length *l* and format *m*:

    l: **b**   One byte.
              h   Two bytes.
              l   Four bytes.

    m: **a**   Characters starting at variable's address.
            c   Character.
            d   Decimal.
            f   32-bit floating.
            g   64-bit double precision floating.
            i   Machine language instruction.
            I   Machine language instruction with numerical address.
            o   Octal.
            p   Pointer to procedure.
            s   Print characters starting at address pointed to by variable.
            u   Unsigned decimal.
            x   Hexadecimal.

linenumber? lm *variable:? lm*	Print from **a.out** and procedure *variable* according to length *l* and format *m*.
variable=lm *linenumber=lm* *number=lm*	Print the address of *variable* or *linenumber*, in the format specified by *l* and *m*. Use the last form to convert *number* to the format specified by *l* and *m*.
variable! value	Assign *value* to *variable*.
x	Display the machine registers and the machine instructions.
X	Display the machine instructions.

Examining the Source:

Command	Function
e*name*	Set the procedure, file, or directory name.
p	Display the current line.
z	Display the current line and several following lines.
w	Display the lines around the current line.
/*regular expression*/	Search ahead for the specified *regular expression*.
?*regular expression*?	Search back for the specified *regular expression*.
number	Make *number* the current line.
count+	Advance *count* lines.
count-	Go back *count* lines.

Executing the Source:

Command	Function
count r *args*	Run the program with the specified arguments. Ignore *count* breakpoints.
count R	Run the program with the no arguments. Ignore *count* breakpoints.
level v	Verbose mode toggle. *level* values 1= source level, 2= assembler level.
linenumber a	Set a breakpoint at *linenumber* and inform the user.
linenumber b *commands*	Set breakpoint at *linenumber* and optionally execute command at breakpoint.
linenumber c *count*	Continue after a breakpoint or ignore *count* breakpoints then stop. If *linenumber* is specified set a temporary breakpoint at *linenumber*.
linenumber C *count*	Continue after a breakpoint (with the halt signal reactivated) or ignore *count* breakpoints then stop. If *linenumber* is specified set a temporary breakpoint at *linenumber*.
linenumber d	Delete breakpoint at *linenumber*.
linenumber g *count*	Continue at *linenumber* after a breakpoint.
procedure (*arg1,arg2,* . . .)	Execute *procedure*.
procedure (*arg1,arg2,* . . .)/*m*	Execute procedure and print result in format *m*.
variable$m *count*	Single step until *variable* is modified.

Miscellaneous Commands:

Command	Function
!cmd	Execute *cmd* with *sh*.
Newline	Display the next line or memory location.
CTRL-D	Scroll the display.
<*file*	Execute the commands contained in *file*.
string	Print *string*.

Breakpoint and Program Control

Command	Function
B	Display the active breakpoints.
D	Remove all breakpoints.
i	Single step mode.
I	Single step with the halt signal activated.
k	Kill the program.
l	Display the last line executed.
M	Display the address map.
M [?/][*]*b e f*	Record new values for the address map.
q	Exit.
s*count*	Single step *count* lines.
S*count*	Single step *count* procedures.
address:**m***count*	Single step until *address* is modified.

Debugging the Debugger:

Command	Function
V	Display the version number.
Q	Display a list of procedures and files being debugged.
Y	Toggle debug output.

Debugging

9

SCCS and Make

The UNIX operating system earned its reputation above all by providing an unexcelled environment for software development. The **make** and SCCS utilities are widely regarded as the greatest contributors to the efficiency of this environment.

The **make** program performs automatic update of a group of interrelated programs. The SCCS system allows all changes to the source code to be recorded, preventing the confusion that may arise from simply saving multiple versions of a source file.

SCCS/Make

SCCS

The Source Code Control System (SCCS) makes it possible for a user to keep track of each revision of a document, avoiding the confusion that often arises from having several versions of one file on line. It is particularly useful when enhancements are made to a program, but the original may still be useful to keep around. Each time a file is "entered" into SCCS, SCCS makes note of which lines have been changed or deleted since the most previous version, and from that information can regenerate the file on demand. Each set of changes is dependent on all previous sets of changes.

Each set of changes is called a "delta", and is assigned a SCCS identification string (*sid*). The *sid* consists of either two components, release and level numbers (in the form *a.b*), or of four components: the release, level, branch, and sequence numbers (in the form *a.b.c.d*). The branches and sequences are for situations when two on-running versions of the same file are recorded in SCCS. For example, *delta 3.2.1.1* refers to release 3, level 2, branch 1, sequence 1.

The SCCS file which holds all the changes must be prefixed by "**s.**".

See Section 1 for syntax lines and options for SCCS commands.

Creating a SCCS File

The **admin** command with the **-i** option creates and initializes SCCS files. For example,

> **admin -ich01 s.ch01**

creates a new SCCS file and initializes it with the contents of **ch01**, which will become *delta 1.1*. The message, "No id keywords (cm7)" appears if you do not specify any keywords. In general, "id keywords" refer to variables in the files that are replaced with appropriate values by **get**, identifying the date and time of creation, the version retrieved, etc. A listing of identification keywords occurs later in this section.

Once the **s.ch01** file is created, the original file **ch01** can be removed, since it can be easily regenerated with the **get** command.

Retrieving a File

The **get** command can retrieve any version of a file from SCCS. Using the example above, you can retrieve **ch01** by entering

> **get -e s.ch01**

and the messages

```
1.1
new delta 1.2
272 lines
```

may appear. This indicates that you are "getting" *delta 1.1*, and the resulting file has 272 lines of text. When the file is reentered into the SCCS file **s.ch01** with the **delta** command, its changes are *delta 1.2*.

The **-e** option indicates to SCCS that you intend to make more changes to the file and then reenter it into SCCS. Without this option, you will receive the file with read-only permissions. The **-e** option, besides releasing the file with read-write permissions, also creates a file **p.ch01**, which records information that will be used by SCCS when the file is returned.

Creating New Releases and Branches

The **-r** option to **get** tells SCCS what release and level number you want, but if no level is specified it defaults to the highest level available. With the command

> **get -r3.2 ch01**

delta 3.2 will be the release. However, the command

> **get -r3 ch01**

returns the highest-numbered level in release 3, for example **3.8**. With the **-r** option omitted, **get** defaults to the highest release, highest level — in other words, the latest version.

When major changes are in store for a file, you may want to begin a new release of the file. You can do that by "getting" the file with the next highest release number. For example, if the latest release of a file is 3.2, and you want to start release 4, enter:

> **get -e -r4 ch01**

You will receive the message,

```
3.2
new delta 4.1
53 lines
```

If you want to make a change to an older version of the same file, you can enter:

> **get -e -r2.2 ch01**

and receive the message:

```
2.2
new delta 2.2.1.1
121 lines
```

You have now created a new branch from the trunk, stemming from version 2.2. Changes in this delta will not affect those in the trunk deltas, i.e., 2.3, 3.1, etc.

Recording Changes

Once changes have been made to the SCCS file, return it to SCCS with the command:

delta s.ch01

You are prompted for comments on the changes. The **delta** command then does its own **get** and compares the new version of the file with the most recent previous version with the **diff** command. It then outputs messages giving the new release number, and how many lines were inserted, deleted, and unchanged.

SCCS Commands

File arguments to SCCS commands can be either filenames or the names of directories; naming a directory will cause all the files in that directory to be processed, with nonapplicable and nonreadable files ignored. If in place of a file argument a ''-'' is entered, the command will read from standard input for the names of files to be processed, one on each line.

Error messages produced by aborted SCCS commands are of the form

ERROR *filename*: *message* (*code*)

The *code* is useful for using the **help** command to find out what the nature of your error was, by entering, ''help *code*''.

Commands for the administration of SCCS are as follows:

get	Retrieve versions of SCCS files.
delta	Create a new version of an SCCS file (i.e., append a new *delta*).
admin	Create new SCCS files and change their parameters.
prs	Print portions of SCCS files in a specified format.
help	Clarify diagnostic messages.
rmdel	Remove an accidental *delta* from an SCCS file.
cdc	Change the comment associated with a *delta*.
what	Search for all occurrences of the pattern **get** substitutes for %Z%, and print out the following text.
sccsdiff	Show the difference between any two SCCS files.
comb	Combine consecutive deltas into a single delta.
val	Validate a SCCS file.

See Section 1 for command lines and options.

──Identification Keywords──────────────────────

The following keywords may be used in an SCCS file:

%M%	module name.
%I%	*sid* of the retrieved text.
%R%	release number.
%L%	level number.
%B%	branch number.
%S%	sequence number.
%D%	current date (YY/MM/DD).
%H%	current date (MM/DD/YY).
%T%	current time (HH:MM:SS).
%E%	date newest applied delta was created (YY/MM/DD).
%G%	date newest applied delta was created (MM/DD/YY).
%U%	time newest applied delta was created (HH:MM:SS).
%Y%	module type, as defined by **admin -ft***type*.
%F%	SCCS file name.
%P%	fully qualified SCCS file name.
%Q%	the value of *string*, as defined by **admin -fq***string*.
%C%	current line number, intended for identifying where error occurred.
%Z%	the string recognized by **what**.
%W%, %A%	shorthand for providing **what** strings for program files.

Data keywords specify which parts of an SCCS file are to be retrieved and output using the **-d** option of the **prs** command.

:Dt:	Delta information.	**:Z:**	**what** string delimiter.
:DL:	Delta line statistics.	**:F:**	SCCS file name.
:Li:	lines inserted by delta.	**:PN:**	SCCS file pathname.
:Ld:	lines deleted by delta.	**:MR:**	modification numbers
:Lu:	lines unchanged by delta.		for delta.
:DT:	delta type.	**:C:**	comments for delta.
:I:	SCCS id string (sid).	**:UN:**	user names.
:R:	release number.	**:FL:**	flag list.
:L:	level number.	**:Y:**	module type flag.
:B:	branch number.	**:MF:**	modification valida-
:S:	sequence number.		tion flag.
:D:	date delta created.	**:MP:**	modification valida-
:Dy:	year delta created.		tion pgm name.
:Dm:	month delta created.	**:KF:**	keyword
:Dd:	day delta created.		error/warning flag.
:T:	time delta created.	**:BF:**	branch flag.
:Th:	hour delta created.	**:J:**	joint edit flag.
:Tm:	minutes delta created.	**:LK:**	locked releases.
:Ts:	seconds delta created.	**:Q:**	user-defined keyword.
:P:	programmer who created	**:M:**	module name.
	delta.	**:CB:**	ceiling boundary.
:DS:	delta sequence number.	**:FB:**	floor boundary.
:DP:	predecessor delta sequence	**:Ds:**	default sid.
	number.	**:FD:**	file descriptive text.
:DI:	sequence number of deltas.	**:ND:**	null delta flag.
:Dn:	deltas included (sequence	**:GB:**	gotten body.
	number).	**:BD:**	body.
:Dx:	deltas excluded (sequence	**:A:**	a form of **what**
	number).		string.
:Dg:	deltas ignored (sequence	**:W:**	a form of **what**
	number).		string.

The **make** program generates a sequence of commands for execution by the UNIX shell. It uses a table of file dependencies input by the programmer, and with this information, can perform updating tasks automatically for the user. It can keep track of the sequence of commands that create certain files, and the list of files that require other files to be current before they can operate efficiently. When a change is made to a program, the **make** command will create the proper files with a minimum of effort.

For a detailed description of **make**, refer to the Nutshell Handbook, *Managing Projects With Make.*

See Section 1 for the syntax and options for **make**.

Internal Macros

$?   The list of components that have been changed more recently than the current target. Can be used only in normal description file entries — not suffix rules.

$@   The name of the current target, except in description file entries for making libraries, where it becomes the library name. Can be used both in normal description file entries and suffix rules.

$<   The name of the current component which has been modified more recently than the current target. Can be used only in suffix rules and the .DEFAULT: entry.

$*   The name — without the suffix — of the current component that has been modified more recently than the current target. Can be used only in suffix rules.

$$@   The name of the current target. Can be used only to the right of the colon in dependency lines.

$%   The name of the corresponding .o file when the current target is a library module. Can be used both in normal description file entries and suffix rules.

Macro Modifiers

D   The directory portion of any internal macro name except $?. For example, $(*D), $(<D), $(@D), $$(@D).

F   The file portion of any internal macro name except $?. For example, $(*F), $(<F), $(@F), $$(@F).

SCCS/Make

Macro String Substitution

$(macro:abc=xyz)
> Evaluates to the current definition of $(macro), after substituting the string **xyz** for every occurrence of **abc** that occurs either immediately before a blank or tab, or at the end of the macro definition.

Pseudo-Targets

.DEFAULT: Commands associated with this pseudo-target will be executed if a legitimate target must be made but there are no applicable description file entries or suffix rules.

.IGNORE: Ignore error codes. Same as the -I option flag.

.PRECIOUS: Components you specify for this pseudo-target will not be removed when you send a signal (such as interrupt) that aborts **make**.

.SILENT: Execute commands but do not echo them. Same as the -s option flag.

Description File Command Codes

@ Do not echo this command line.

- Ignore error return from this command.

Sample Default Macros, Suffixes, and Rules

```
EDITOR = /usr/bin/vi
TERM = tvi950ns
SHELL = /bin/csh
PATH = .:/bin:/usr/bin:/usr/fred:/usr/local
LOGNAME = fred
HOME = /usr/fred
GFLAGS =
GET = get
ASFLAGS =
AS = as
FFLAGS =
FC = f77
CFLAGS = -O
CC = cc
LDFLAGS =
LD = ld
LFLAGS =
LEX = lex
YFLAGS =
YACC = yacc
MAKE = make
$ = $
MAKEFLAGS = b
```

```
.h~.h:
     $(GET) $(GFLAGS) -p $< > $*.h

.s~.a:
     $(GET) $(GFLAGS) -p $< > $*.s
     $(AS) $(ASFLAGS) -o $*.o $*.s
     ar rv $@ $*.o
     -rm -f $*.[so]

.r~.a:
     $(GET) $(GFLAGS) -p $< > $*.r
     $(FC) -c $(FFLAGS) $*.r
     ar rv $@ $*.o
     rm -f $*.[ro]

.e~.a:
     $(GET) $(GFLAGS) -p $< > $*.e
     $(FC) -c $(FFLAGS) $*.e
     ar rv $@ $*.o
     rm -f $*.[eo]

.f~.a:
     $(GET) $(GFLAGS) -p $< > $*.f
     $(FC) -c $(FFLAGS) $*.f
     ar rv $@ $*.o
     rm -f $*.[fo]

.r.a:
     $(FC) -c $(FFLAGS) $<
     ar rv $@ $*.o
     rm -f $*.o

.e.a:
     $(FC) -c $(FFLAGS) $<
     ar rv $@ $*.o
     rm -f $*.o

.f.a:
     $(FC) -c $(FFLAGS) $<
     ar rv $@ $*.o
     rm -f $*.o

.c~.a:
     $(GET) $(GFLAGS) -p $< > $*.c
     $(CC) -c $(CFLAGS) $*.c
     ar rv $@ $*.o
     rm -f $*.[co]

.c.a:
     $(CC) -c $(CFLAGS) $<
     ar rv $@ $*.o
     rm -f $*.o
```

```
.l.c:
        $(LEX) $<
        mv lex.yy.c $@

.y~.c:
        $(GET) $(GFLAGS) -p $< > $*.y
        $(YACC) $(YFLAGS) $*.y
        mv y.tab.c $*.c
        -rm -f $*.y

.y.c:
        $(YACC) $(YFLAGS) $<
        mv y.tab.c $@

.l~.o:
        $(GET) $(GFLAGS) -p $< > $*.l
        $(LEX) $(LFLAGS) $*.l
        $(CC) $(CFLAGS) -c lex.yy.c
        rm -f lex.yy.c $*.l
        mv lex.yy.o $*.o

.l.o:
        $(LEX) $(LFLAGS) $<
        $(CC) $(CFLAGS) -c lex.yy.c
        rm lex.yy.c
        mv lex.yy.o $@

.y~.o:
        $(GET) $(GFLAGS) -p $< > $*.y
        $(YACC) $(YFLAGS) $*.y
        $(CC) $(CFLAGS) -c y.tab.c
        rm -f y.tab.c $*.y
        mv y.tab.o $*.o

.y.o:
        $(YACC) $(YFLAGS) $<
        $(CC) $(CFLAGS) -c y.tab.c
        rm y.tab.c
        mv y.tab.o $@

.s~.o:
        $(GET) $(GFLAGS) -p $< > $*.s
        $(AS) $(ASFLAGS) -o $*.o $*.s
        -rm -f $*.s

.s.o:
        $(AS) $(ASFLAGS) -o $@ $<

.r~.o:
        $(GET) $(GFLAGS) -p $< > $*.r
        $(FC) $(FFLAGS) -c $*.r
        -rm -f $*.r
```

The MAKE Utility

```
.e~.e:
        $(GET) $(GFLAGS) -p $< > $*.e

.e~.o:
        $(GET) $(GFLAGS) -p $< > $*.e
        $(FC) $(FFLAGS) -c $*.e
        -rm -f $*.e

.f~.f:
        $(GET) $(GFLAGS) -p $< > $*.f

.f~.o:
        $(GET) $(GFLAGS) -p $< > $*.f
        $(FC) $(FFLAGS) -c $*.f
        -rm -f $*.f

.r.o:
        $(FC) $(FFLAGS) -c $<

.e.o:
        $(FC) $(FFLAGS) -c $<

.f.o:
        $(FC) $(FFLAGS) -c $<

.c~.c:
        $(GET) $(GFLAGS) -p $< > $*.c

.c~.o:
        $(GET) $(GFLAGS) -p $< > $*.c
        $(CC) $(CFLAGS) -c $*.c
        -rm -f $*.c

.c.o:
        $(CC) $(CFLAGS) -c $<

.sh~:
        $(GET) $(GFLAGS) -p $< > $*.sh
        cp $*.sh $*
        -rm -f $*.sh

.sh:
        cp $< $@

.r~:
        $(GET) $(GFLAGS) -p $< > $*.r
        $(FC) -n $(FFLAGS) $*.r -o $*
        -rm -f $*.r

.r:
        $(FC) $(FFLAGS) $(LDFLAGS) $< -o $@

.e~:
        $(GET) $(GFLAGS) -p $< > $*.e
        $(FC) -n $(FFLAGS) $*.e -o $*
```

```
      -rm -f $*.e
.e:
      $(FC) $(FFLAGS) $(LDFLAGS) $< -o $@
.f~:
      $(GET) $(GFLAGS) -p $< > $*.f
      $(FC) -n $(FFLAGS) $*.f -o $*
      -rm -f $*.f
.f:
      $(FC) $(FFLAGS) $(LDFLAGS) $< -o $@
.c~:
      $(GET) $(GFLAGS) -p $< > $*.c
      $(CC) -n $(CFLAGS) $*.c -o $*
      -rm -f $*.c
.c:
      $(CC) $(CFLAGS) $(LDFLAGS) $< -o $@
.SUFFIXES:
      .o  .c  .c~  .f  .f~  .e  .e~  .r  .r~
      .y  .y~  .l  .l~  .s  .s~  .sh  .sh~  .h  .h~
```